BYRON IN LOVE

BYRON IN LOVE

A Short Daring Life

EDNA O'BRIEN

W. W. Norton & Company
New York • London

First American Edition 2009

Printed in the United States of America

For information about permission to reproduce selections from
this book, write to Permissions, W. W. Norton & Company, Inc.,
500 Fifth Avenue, New York, NY 10110

For information about special discounts for bulk purchases,
please contact W. W. Norton Special Sales at
specialsales@wwnorton.com or 800-233-4830

Manufacturing by Courier Westford
Production manager: Anna Oler

Library of Congress Cataloging-in-Publication Data

O'Brien, Edna.
Byron in love : a short daring life / Edna O'Brien. — 1st American ed.
p. cm.
ISBN 978-0-393-07011-8 (hardcover)
1. Byron, George Gordon Byron, Baron, 1788-1824. 2. Poets, English—
19th century—Biography. I. Title.
PR4381.O47 2009
821'.7—dc22
[B] 2009007109

W. W. Norton & Company, Inc.
500 Fifth Avenue, New York, N.Y. 10110
www.wwnorton.com

W. W. Norton & Company Ltd.
Castle House, 75/76 Wells Street, London W1T 3QT

1 2 3 4 5 6 7 8 9 0

For Ann Getty –
a Byron admirer

'In the career of writing, a man should calculate upon his powers of resistance before he goes into the arena.'

LORD BYRON – *LETTER TO SHELLEY*, 1821

'Everything connected with the life and character of so illustrious a bard as the late Lord Byron is public property.'

J. MITFORD – *LES AMOURS SECRETES DE LORD BYRON*, 1839

'But words are things, and a small drop of ink,
Falling like dew upon a thought, produces
That which makes thousands, perhaps millions, think.'

LORD BYRON – *DON JUAN* III.88

'The more Byron is known, the better he will be loved.'

TERESA GUICCIOLI, 1873, on her death bed

ACKNOWLEDGEMENTS

Byron left a great and enduring portrait of himself to posterity, in his *Letters and Journals*, edited first by R.E. Prothero (1898) and more extensively by Leslie A. Marchand (1973–4). Professor Marchand's three-volume *Life of Byron* (1957) is essential reading for all Byron aspirants.

I am also deeply grateful to a host of other authors – biographers, scholars, poets and yes, even scoundrels, who have written with passion, erudition and far-fetchedness, yet the relationship with their subject always fascinating and symbiotic, while being sometimes territorial. They include Tom Moore, R.C. Dallas, John Galt, John Cam Hobhouse, Thomas Medwin, Edward Trelawny, Leigh Hunt, William Parry, Colonel Stanhope, Julius Millingen, Count Pietro Gamba, Teresa Guiccioli, John William Polidori, Samuel Rogers, John Mitford, George Ticknor, John Drinkwater, Ralph Milbanke Lovelace, André Maurois, Harriet Beecher Stowe, Ethel Colburn Mayne, Malcolm Elwin, Iris Origo, Thomas Macaulay, Lady Blessington, Harriette Wilson, George Patson, Peter Quennell, Harold Nicolson, Michael Foot, Jerome J. McGann, Doris Langley Moore, Elizabeth Longford, Anne Barton, W.H. Auden, Phyllis Grosskurth, Benita Eisler, Fiona MacCarthy, Megan Boyes, Anne Fleming,

Michael and Melissa Bakewell, Kay Redfield Jamison. I also consulted journals and periodicals of the time.

The wonderful staff at the London Library and the British Library were untiring in their help.

INTRODUCTION

In his seminal essay on Shakespeare's *Antony and Cleopatra*, Harold Bloom cites Cleopatra as 'the archetype of the star and the world's first celebrity', one who eclipsed her lovers, Pompey, Caesar and Antony, never straying from the empiric necessity of playing herself. Byron must surely rank as her counterpart in life, the first and ongoing celebrity, hero and villain, wooer and narcissist, shackled with a label that has entered everyday currency of being 'mad, bad and dangerous to know'.

It is the same Byron who wrote –

> What is the end of fame? 'Tis but to fill
> A certain portion of uncertain paper
> . . .
> For this men write, speak, preach, and heroes kill,
> And bards burn what they call their midnight taper,
> To have, when the original is dust,
> A name, a wretched picture and worse bust.

There is a legion of books, treatises, essays and biographies on Lord Byron – scholarly, probing, affectionate, discursive, titillating, scurrilous and fantastical, some raising him to an apotheosis and others consigning him to the gutter. Professor Leslie Marchand's biography, published in 1957, was Herculean, unearthing much that was hidden and debunking some of the more preposterous claims and fancies.

So why another book on Byron?

Years ago, reading a remark of Lady Blessington that Byron was 'the most extraordinary and terrifying person [she had] ever met' whetted my interest. Writers writing about other artists has always appealed to me – Rilke on Rodin, addressing that mysterious mediation between the life and the art. Virginia Woolf's *Common Reader*, providing those quick, deft glimpses that give us the human quotidian and a whiff of the genius within; Hardy watering the ink or Dorothy Wordsworth trudging up a wet road with dear William, to seek out a waterfall.

Similarly with Byron, I wanted to follow him in his Rake's Progress and his Poet's Progress, playing billiards in an English country house and passing clandestine notes to a young bride under the very watch of her pontifical husband, Sir Wedderburn Webster, Byron reading Madame de Staël's *Corinne* in the garden of his Italian mistress and writing her a love letter in English, which neither she nor her jealous husband would understand. Byron in love, Byron seized with melancholia and Byron in intermittent 'phrenzy' with his forbearing publisher John Murray. Byron who mapped for himself a great and tragic destiny, going as he thought 'to the seat of war', when he set out to join in the cause for Greek independence, and instead dying of a fever in a swamp in Missolonghi at the age of thirty-six, the face that had been the Adonis of all Europe covered in leeches and bandages.

So I immersed myself in the twelve volumes of his letters and journals, in which he variously reveals himself as a passionate man, an intellectual man, a wounded man, a jesting man and the archetype for Napoleon, Don Quixote, Don Juan, Richard Lovelace, Richard III, Richard II and ultimately a Lear surrounded by knaves and fools. I read the numerous biographies of him and those of Lady Byron, the histrionic accounts of a marriage of just over one year, that not only served as fascination for the tabloids and cartoonists of his time, but even intrigued such an elevated mind as Goethe's.

Byron with his odes and his dithyrambics, his scoffing at *litteratoor*, coupled with his lifelong service to it, his banter and colloquy with men and women, his excruciating dissection of his own delinquencies, proved to be a very great and unnerving companion.

ONE

Lord George Gordon Byron was five feet eight and a half inches in height, had a malformed right foot, chestnut hair, a haunting pallor, temples of alabaster, teeth like pearls, grey eyes fringed with dark lashes and an enchantedness that neither men nor women could resist. Everything about him was a paradox, insider and outsider, beautiful and deformed, serious and facetious, profligate but on occasion miserly, and possessed of a fierce intelligence trapped however in a child's magic and malices. What he wrote concerning the poet Robert Burns could easily serve as his own epitaph – 'tenderness, roughness – delicacy, coarseness – sentiment, sensuality . . . dirt and deity – all mixed up in that one compound of inspired clay'.

He was also a gigantic poet, but as he reminds us, poetry is a distinct faculty and has no more to do with the individual than has the pythoness when she is off her tripod. Byron, off his tripod, becomes Byron the Man, who by his own admission could not exist without some object of love. His passions were developed very early and generated excitement, melancholy and foreboding at the loss that was bound to occur in the 'terrestrial paradise'. He loved men and women, needing the 'other', whoever she or he might be. He had only to look at a beautiful face and was ready to 'build and burn another Troy'.

The word Byronic, to this day, connotes excess, diabolical deeds and a rebelliousness answering neither to king nor commoner. Byron, more than any other poet, has come to personify the poet as rebel, imaginative and lawless, reaching beyond race, creed or frontier, his manifest flaws redeemed by a magnetism and ultimately a heroism, that by ending in tragedy, raised it and him from the particular to the universal, from the individual to the archetypal.

TWO

His beginning was not propitious. In January 1788 London was frozen over, frost fires and frost fairs on the Thames for weeks, the severe weather attributed to an Icelandic volcanic eruption. It was in a rented room above a shop in Holles Street, London, to which the 22-year-old mother, Catherine Gordon, had repaired for her accouchement, attended by a midwife, a nurse and a doctor. The labour was tortuous, the infant born with a caul over his face, a supposed emblem of good luck; alarm however at discovering that he had a club foot.

The father, 'Mad Jack' Byron, was not present because had he returned to England he would have been imprisoned for debt. Mr Hanson, a young solicitor, had been dispatched by Catherine's trustees from Aberdeen as a sign of solidarity for the mother, alone in London without her vagrant husband. The foot was contracted to a stump, the lower calf wasted and thin, an affliction that would bring torment, derision and humiliation to the future young Lord, fitted as he was with leg irons, trusses and various contraptions down the years on the advice of quacks and orthopaedic doctors. Various causes for the deformity had been suggested, including a deprivation of oxygen to the lungs, but Byron ever quick to castigate his mother would put it down to her vanity in wearing a too-tight corset during pregnancy.

For him, the lame foot would become the mark of Cain, a symbol of castration and a stigma that blighted his life.

Money, or rather the acute shortage of money, dominated the minds of both parents in those wintry weeks. Writing from France to his sister Frances Leigh in England, Mad Jack, in dire need of money, added that as for his son's walking ''tis impossible for he is clubfooted'. Catherine herself was pressing the executor of her trustees in Edinburgh, outlining her straits, adding that the twenty guineas they had sent her for her accouchement was not enough and she was in need of one hundred guineas. She hoped as well that the rakish and reckless husband would reappear and that mother, father and infant could repair to somewhere in Wales or the north of England, where they might live cheaply, the fleeting happiness of her courtship in Bath a mere three years earlier rekindled. Her hopes were futile. After two months she was writing again to the executor in Edinburgh, her plaints more extreme – 'Leave this House I must in a fortnight from this day so there is no time to be lost and if they will not remit the money before that time I don't know what I shall do and what will become of me.'

The child had been christened George Gordon, named after her father, in Marylebone Church, which had served as an interior for scenes in Hogarth's *Rake's Progress*. The high-born but estranged Scottish relatives, the Duke of Gordon and Colonel Robert Duff of Fetteresso, named as godparents, were sadly absent. Catherine was a descendant of Sir William Gordon and Annabella Stuart, daughter of King James I. The Gordons of Gight were feudal barons who had kept the north country in terror and bondage, begetting illegitimate children, raping and plundering. Some were executed on the scaffold, some were murdered and some died at their own hands. Her grandfather had thrown himself in the icy Ythan River, just below the walls of the castle of Gight, and her father's body had been found floating in the Bath Canal. Her mother had died young, as had her two sisters, leaving Catherine sole heir to a fortune worth thirty thousand pounds' income a year from shares in vast tracts of lands, the Bank of Aberdeen salmon-fishing rights and the rent from coalmines.

At the age of twenty she had gone to Bath, one of the many expectant heiresses in search of a husband. She was not beautiful and according to Byron's friend and first revering biographer Tom Moore, she was short, corpulent and 'rolled in her gait'. She had little intellectual prowess to compensate for that plainness. Also, she was impressionable and seemingly had had a presentiment, because a year earlier at a theatre in Scotland, when the famous actress Mrs Siddons in a play called *The Fatal Marriage* exclaimed 'Oh my Biron, my Biron', Catherine's hysterics were such that she had to be carried from her box. In Bath she met her 'Biron', Mad Jack, recently widowed and broke. He had previously wooed Amelia, the enchanting wife of the Marquis of Carmarthen, who eloped with him to France, her fortune, along with her health, soon to be ruined by his profligacy and philandering. His courtship of Catherine was soon accomplished. Her Scottish cousins, knowing her to be impetuous and probably guessing that the future husband was a bounder, tried to persuade her against the marriage but she was adamant and she was besotted.

They married, went back to the castle of Gight, where Jack orchestrated a life of grandeur, horses and hounds, gambling, excesses so ostentatious that they were famed in a ballad. On a hurried visit to London in the same year as their marriage,

Jack was seized for debt and taken to the King's Bench Prison, his tailor being the only person in the vicinity able to bail him out. Soon, like many debtors, the married couple fled to France, the money gone, the castle and much of the estate sold to a cousin of Catherine's, Lord Aberdeen, and the young wife not only without her kin but destitute of their respect for having come down so shamefully in the world.

Byron barely saw his father and yet, all his life, he was in thrall to the colourful and daring exploits of his paternal ancestors, born and bred in arms, having led their vassals, as he boasted, from Europe to Palestine's plains. The vivid narrative of a shipwreck off the coast of Arracan written by an ancestor provided the stimulus and inspiration for Canto Four of *Don Juan*. With regard to his mother's family, he would be more judgemental, going so far as to claim that all bad blood in him had derived from those bastards of Banquo.

As Tom Moore tells us 'disappointment met him on the very threshold of life' – a mother quick-tempered and capricious, the softening influences of a sister denied him. Moore says that he was deprived of the solaces that might have brought down the high current of his feelings and 'saved them from the tumultous rapids and falls'. Except that these selfsame rapids and falls characterised his ancestors on both sides. The Byrons, mentioned in the Domesday Book, were the de Buruns of Normandy, liegemen of William the Conqueror, reaping titles and lands in Nottinghamshire, Derbyshire and Lancashire for their prowess in land and sea battles. A John Byron of Colwyke, in the year 1573, acquired Newstead Abbey in Nottinghamshire from Henry VIII, the house, church and cloisters, on three thousand acres of grounds, for the sum of £810, and was knighted by Queen Elizabeth I some six years later. He remodelled Newstead to suit his secular and lavish tastes, even installing his own resident troupe of players. At Byron's birth his grand-uncle, known as the Wicked Lord, was living in seclusion at Newstead, the family seat. He had been a wild man, but with life's vicissitudes he had grown reclusive. He built a folly castle and stone forts on the lake that were fitted with a fleet of toy ships, where he conducted naval battles with his servant Joe Murray, who had to act as factotum and second officer and was said to have taught the crickets in the chimneypiece to speak back to him.

In 1765, in a tavern in Pall Mall in London, the squires and nobles of Nottinghamshire, many of them relatives, had assembled for a levee. The Wicked Lord and his cousin, William Chaworth, fell into an argument on how best to hang game; the acrimony became so extreme that the two men repaired to an upper room, where by the light of a single candle the Wicked Lord plunged his shortsword through the belly of his opponent. He spent a brief spell in the Tower of London for murder before being pardoned by his fellow peers and was discharged after paying a modest fee. The Wicked Lord returned to Newstead, became increasingly embittered, his wife having left him; he begot a child by one of the servants who gave herself the pseudonym of Lady Betty. His son and heir William was due to marry an heiress but instead eloped with a first cousin and, in spite, the Wicked Lord had the great oak woods stripped and the two thousand deer that roamed the woods were slaughtered and sold at Mansfield market for a pittance. In a last spree of vengeance, he leased the rights of coalmines he owned in Rochdale, depriving all future heirs of their income. Yet, Byron would boast of the nobility of his lineage, forgetting to add that many of them were brutes, vagabonds, given to episodic madness, and as

Thomas Moore put it, never free from 'the inroads of financial embarrassment'.

In August, when Mad Jack had not returned to complete the family tableau, Catherine and her infant son set out on the public coach for Aberdeen and once again she was obliged to take rooms above a shop. Her husband did appear from time to time, to extract money from a woman whose income was now reduced to £150 a year. The vicious rows that ensued and that Byron claimed to remember left him, as he put it, 'with little taste for matrimony'.

Life in Aberdeen for mother and son was spartan and somewhat volatile, Catherine a woman of extremes, veering from excessive affection to bouts of anger, her son retaliating with his own unfettered temper, neighbours recalling how Mrs Byron would take the tongs to him, brand him a 'cripple' and five minutes later smother him with kisses. For his part, he amused himself at church services by sticking a safety-pin in his mother's plump arms. He refused to be subdued. Dressed in the Gordon tartans of blue and green, he rode a pony, carried a whip and if his lameness was mocked, as it frequently was, he wielded the whip with 'Dinnya speak of it'.

From France, Mad Jack pleaded with his sister Frances, who had also been his lover, 'for God's sake to come' as he had no bed, no person to care for him and was living on scraps. In August 1791 he died of consumption in Valenciennes, having dictated a will to two notaries leaving the three-year-old son responsible for his debts and funeral expenses, which Catherine managed to discharge by borrowing on a legacy of just over one thousand pounds, which she was due to receive on the death of her grandmother. When she learnt of her husband's death, her screams were heard down the length of Broad Street, her grief 'bordering on distraction'. In a fairly imperious letter to her sister-in-law, whom she addressed as 'My dear Madam', she emphasised her great grief, then requesting a lock of his hair, she reiterated the love between herself and her 'dear Jonnie'.

At five and a half, Byron had become so unruly that Catherine sent him to school in the hope that he could be kept 'in abeyance'. Schisms and tempers at home, Catherine referring to him as that 'lame brat', the castigation so etched in his memory that years later in a drama, *The Deformed Transformed*, Arnold the hunchback is addressed by his mother as an incubus and a nightmare, as he pleads with her not to kill him, while hating his vile form.

Under the tutelage of a Mr Bowers he quickly developed a passion for history, especially Roman history, revelling in the stories of battle and shipwreck, which he would later enact for himself. When he was six he was translating Horace, reading the great but grave accounts of death, how death made itself felt in palace halls and in huts, his imagination fearfully quickened. Before he was eight years old he had read all the books of the Old Testament, finding the New Testament not nearly so rich in description. When he was enrolled in a grammar school, he reckoned, though we must allow for some boyish exaggeration, that he had read four thousand works of fiction, his favourites being Cervantes, Smollett and Scott. But history was his greatest passion and Knolles's *Turkish History* would incite the hunger to visit the Levant as a young man and provide the exotic background for many of his oriental tales.

It was at a dancing school, aged eight, that he was smitten by the charms of Mary Duff and though he did not know it by name, felt the attendant joys and uncertainty of first rapturous love. Mary was one of those evanescent beings, made of rainbow, with a Greek cast of features, to whom he would for ever be susceptible, her successor being a distant cousin, Margaret Parker, for whom he also conceived a violent love. That twin soul he sought again and again in blood relatives, passions by which he would be thrown into 'convulsive confusion'. The antithesis to such tenderness was his countering cruelty. He had a fascination for a gothic novel, *Zeluco*, in which the anti-hero was fated to commit crimes he could not control, strangling those closest to him, taming a pet sparrow in order to be able to wring its neck, dark deeds that instead of consigning him to the dungeons, elevated him to the status of Magus, which Byron himself would aspire to.

There was no fraternising with the Byron family, though Catherine tried to enlist Frances Leigh to get financial help from the Wicked Lord – 'You know Lord Byron. Do you think he will do anything for George or be at any expense to give him a proper education or if he wished to do it, is his present fortune such a one that he could spare anything out of it?' Each letter was ignored. Then one morning in 1798 news reached them that the Wicked Lord had died, aged sixty-five, his son William Byron already having been killed in Corsica by a cannonball at the Battle of Calvi in 1794. The ten-year-old George became the sixth Lord Byron, an ennoblement by which mother and son were briefly borne on wings of Icarus.

The whole cosmos of Byron's childhood was altered. He would be given wine and cake by the headmaster at his grammar school and yield to a bout of tears when at the roll call, instead of Byron, he answered Dominus de Byron, and when the looking glass failed to reveal a different him, he determined to become different within and acquit himself like a lord. For his mother also it was a dizzying ascent into a new world, the move down to England would be dislocating, her new friends would be Byron relatives and in time she would become her son's minion and a tenant in her son's house.

Her first appearance at the Abbey did not impress the toll mistress, who thought her slovenly and also thought that the boy was far too plump to be sitting on the lap of his nurse, May Gray. Catherine had had to sell her furniture to help towards the funeral of the Wicked Lord, who lay for weeks in the Abbey as creditors seized whatever they could. Her effects yielded £74 17s 6d and her one somewhat lofty request was that the Newstead servants wear black at the funeral. When by the end of August 1798 she had accrued enough money, she set out for the 377-mile journey, on the public stagecoach, with Byron and May Gray; the three-day journey entailed stops at the very unprepossessing inns that her meagre funds would allow.

THREE

Scotch plaids, Scotch snoods, the Scottish burr, blue hills and deep-black salmon streams were no more. Instead an ancestral seat, the twelfth-century monastery flanked by buildings from later centuries, some ramshackle and open to the sky, yet the effect can only have been that of wonder to such a susceptible trio, mother and son shedding (as they would have thought) the gloom and stigma of rented rooms for such inestimable grandeur. Newstead Abbey, a massive structure of grey granite, with Gothic arches and Gothic windows, the scene of orgies and rituals, and was said to be presided over by the ghost of a black-hooded monk who stalked the empty galleries at night, avenging the crime of its being converted from a place of worship to a place of hedonism.

Inside, haunted rooms, vaulted passages, a cloister and an armoire, where some of the Wicked Lord's pistols had escaped the clutches of the creditors. In the main bedroom, which Byron promptly assigned to himself, hung the iron sword with which the Wicked Lord had slain his cousin and the family arms depicting a mermaid flanked by two chestnut horses and bearing the motto 'Crede Byron'. Never mind that it was a ruin, one wing open to the sky, the refectory serving as a hayshed, cattle in the cloisters, it was his magic Castle. Joe

Murray, the old truculent servant who had been used to the madman's ways, resented the presence of the hot-tempered mother, who complained about the dirt and disorder, and of the precocious son with his airs. Byron's conduct was that of musts, insisting that he be waited upon, that he be allowed to do pistol shooting, even indoors if he felt like it, and that he be allowed to carry loaded pistols in his waistcoat pockets, a habit which he adopted for life. Furious that the forest had been felled, he planted an acorn and said, somewhat loftily, 'As it prospers, so I shall prosper.'

Annesley Hall, the home of the slain Viscount Chaworth, was joined to Newstead by a long avenue of oaks, known as the Bridal Path, since the third Lord Byron had married Elizabeth, daughter of the Viscount. Mr Hanson, the family lawyer who was to administer the estate, had come from London to welcome them and noting Byron's precociousness, remarked that there lived there a very pretty young cousin called Mary Ann, whom Byron might marry. The crisp rejoinder was – 'What. Mr Hanson? The Capulets and the Montagues intermarry?' Mary Ann would be another of those etherealised beings for whom he would fall into an 'ebullition of passion', except that her sighs were for a Mr Musters, a foxhunting gentleman, rumoured to be the illegitimate son of the Prince Regent, but according to Mary Ann's parents 'a monster of profligacy and depravity'.

He would meet cousins, aunts, great-aunts and by being the only boy among them he was duly spoilt. The first letter that Byron, aged eleven, penned to his Great-aunt Frances Byron Parker-Parkyns is arch and self-possessed:

Dear Madam, – My Mamma being unable to write herself desires I will let you know that the potatoes are now ready and you are welcome to them whenever you please – She begs you will ask Mrs Parkyns if she would wish the poney to go round by Nottingham or go home the nearest way as it is now quite well but too small to carry me – I have sent a young Rabbit which I beg Miss Frances will accept off and which I promised to send before – My Mamma desires her best compliments to you all in which I join – I am, Dear Aunt, Yours Sincerely,

BYRON

I hope you will excuse all blunders as it is the first letter I ever wrote.

By November the Abbey was freezing and damp, so that mother and son had to decamp, Byron with his nurse May Gray to the Parkyns cousins in nearby Southwell and Catherine travelling to London to plead with Mr Hanson to persuade Lord Carlisle, another distant cousin, to become Byron's guardian, a duty he took on most reluctantly. For the period of Byron's minority, Catherine having only £122 per annum of her own, pleaded with Lord Carlisle to use his influence to secure a pension from the Civil List, and so with his influence and the Duke of Portland's, the King ordered the Prime Minister, Mr Pitt, to pay her £300 a year. But it was not enough to restore the Abbey or the outbuildings as she tried helplessly to set new rents for farm tenants and disentangle the legal knots by which the estate was encumbered. He would escape at night to go back and look at Newstead, his lost paradise and the rage at banishment was not dissimilar to that of Heathcliff in *Wuthering Heights*, Byron thought to be the partial inspiration for Emily Brontë's brooding and thwarted hero.

Since the young Parkyns girls received private tuition from

a Mr Dummer Rogers, Byron decided that he must be treated likewise and wrote peremptorily to his mother in London: 'Mr Rogers could attend me every night at a separate hour from the Miss Parkynses . . . I recommend this to you because, if some plan of this kind is not adopted, I shall be called, or rather branded with the name of Dunce, which you know I could never bear.' Byron and Mr Rogers read Virgil and Cicero together, the tutor only too aware that his pupil was in torment from the contraption on his foot, but stoically determined that it should not be mentioned. Mr Lavender, a truss-maker from the General Hospital, who styled himself 'surgeon', had been engaged by Catherine to ensure that Byron would no longer be a 'cripple'. Mr Lavender's course of treatments was primitive, the deformed foot was rubbed with hot oil, then twisted and forced into a wooden contraption, so that Byron was in worse torture. When he came to London a year later and Mr Hanson brought him to a more experienced physician, a Dr Baillie, he must have raged at hearing the two men say that it was in infancy that the malformation should have been treated and so the blame heaped upon his mother was all the more vindictive.

Catherine came to be ostracised by her scornful son, Mr Hanson and his family, the dilettante Lord Carlisle. Dr Glennie, the headmaster at Dr Glennie's academy in Dulwich, to which Byron was admitted at the age of eleven on Carlisle's recommendation. He wrote of her thus – 'Mrs Byron is a total stranger to English society and English manners, with an exterior far from prepossessing, a mind wholly without cultivation and the peculiarities of Northern opinions, Northern habits and Northern accent . . . not a Madame de Lambert endowed with powers to retrieve the fortune and form the character and manners of a young nobleman, her son.' In a world of male sovreignty, poor Catherine did not stand a chance.

When a fellow pupil at Glennie's school had said to him 'Your mother is a fool', Byron's caustic retort was 'I know it but you must not say so'. Her foolishness had become evident for him in her infatuation with a French dancing master, M. de Louis, whom she had met at Brompton, where she had gone to learn a few steps and then unwisely she had brought him to the school on visiting Sunday. Thereafter she was forbidden visits, but she came anyhow, screamed and harangued at the gate, causing Dr Glennie to describe her as one of the Furies. In a letter to his half-sister Augusta born in 1783, the child of Mad Jack and his first wife, Lady Amelia D'Arcy, who had eloped with him, leaving her husband, Lord Carmarthen, Byron sneered at his mother's weakness, a woman who had 'sunk' her age, as he put it, a good six years, averring that she was only eighteen when he was born, whereas in fact she was just twenty-three. They were alike in their burning temperaments and yet unalike, the mother loud, gross-featured and provincial, Byron in dress and in manner already patrician and fastidious. His demands on her were not that of a son but of a tyrannical husband. No captive Negro, he would claim, ever longed for liberation as dearly as he.

'To Harrow Boarding School he went.' Dr Glennie wrote that Byron was 'as little prepared as it is natural to suppose from two years of elementary instruction, thwarted by every art that could estrange the mind of youth from preceptor, from school and from all serious study'. John Cam Hobhouse, who would become Byron's lifelong friend, provided an unvarnished perspective of English boarding schools, describing them as temples of fagging, flogging and homoerotic initiation.

Harrow, a mere twelve miles from London, with a view of Windsor and Oxford in the distance, was the boarding school for prospective dukes, marquises, earls, viscounts, lords, hons and baronets, many of whom were sent there at the tender age of six. Byron was just thirteen when he enrolled, but already he had acquired mastery over his mother, insisting, despite her meagre allowance from Chancery, he be togged out in keeping with his nobility. He had ticking trousers, buckskin breeches, a coat of superfine olive cloth, a new brace for his foot and a special padded built-up boot to hide the unseemliness of his shin.

At first he was made to feel his lameness 'most bitterly', jeered and bullied by older boys, something which in time he would address, by learning to fight, cultivating strength in chest, arms and lungs. The headmaster's wife Mrs Drury recalled 'the lame boy Birron struggling up the hill like a ship in a storm, without rudder or compass'. Her husband however saw that what had been submitted to his tutelage was 'a wild mountain colt', but he also recognised that the young boy had 'mind in his eyes'. Schooling was rigorous, boys at their desks before six in the morning and by the light of a single tallow wick, reading, parsing and memorising the Greek and Latin texts. The classrooms were cold, the oak walls and benches blackened from the fire, birches and flogging stools for miscreants and laggards. Punishment of a more questionable kind featured in the dormitories at night, which were not supervised, boys bathing together and some, for a lesser fee, sharing a bed. Boys blessed with good looks, which certainly Byron was, were accorded female names and chosen as 'bitches' by the bigger boys for their sport. The pleasure of inflicting 'stripes' was a precursor to greater intimacies. Those who declined got a cuffing or a kicking until they submitted. These grosser carryings-on were tempered in daylight with more ideal sentiments, tributes and verses from pupil to pupil. Byron's school friendships were, as he said, 'passions' because of his violent disposition, first for a fellow peer, William Harness, aged ten, also lame, and when that led to estrangement it was John Fitzgibbon, Earl of Clare, whom Byron claimed to love 'ad infinitum', a love interrupted only by distance, claiming he could never hear the word 'Clare' without a murmur of the heart.

At school holidays however his 'passions' branched in the opposite direction, his affections once again centred on Mary Chaworth, and he recalls as it were an epiphany, Mary and he visiting a cave in Derbyshire, lying side by side in a small raft, pushed by a ferryman to whom he gave the incendiary name of Charon, thereby coupling bliss with damnation. No breath, no being, existed for him but hers. His immolation was utter and in a poem, 'The Dream', written thirteen years later, he admitted that he had ceased to live within himself, she was his life, 'the ocean to the river of his thoughts'.

When the time came to return to Harrow, he refused, the letters from him at Annesley, to his mother in Southwell, becoming more and more pleading: 'I only *desire*, *entreat*, this one day, and on my honour I will be over tomorrow . . . Those that I most love live in this County; therefore in the name of Mercy I entreat this one day to take leave . . .' His mother, jealous of this love, would in time take revenge, being the first to give him the intelligence of the wedding between Mr Musters and Miss Chaworth, forewarning him that he might need his handkerchief. A cousin, observing his feigned indifference, saw that he was determined to conceal the wound, but felt bitterness towards Catherine for telling him.

The various wretchednesses and rebuffs had made him more pugilistic and back at Harrow, for the spring term, he was a formidable opponent with his sharp tongue and his strong fists. He gathered around himself a clan, cohorts who would revel in his arrogance and his rebelliousness. Dr Drury was to say Byron spread 'riot and confusion' in the house, and so subversive did his pranks become that for the following term he was suspended and only with the interceding of Lord Carlisle was he ever allowed back.

His letters of those four years, with such a stellar command of language, show him in many alternating moods, precocious, arrogant or suppliant, depending on whom he was writing to. During a school holiday he had met his half-sister Augusta at General Harcourt's house in Portland Place in London, and this languid, amiable girl was soon to become the recipient of a trove of gallant and over-affectionate missives. She was his 'dearest sis', his nearest relative in the world, and he was bound to her by ties of both blood and affection. Ah, how wretched he was at their being hitherto separated, all the jealous work of his mother, whom he depicted as 'a happy compound of derangement and folly'. Catherine was merely necessary to provide money, to go to Mr Sheldrake in the Strand to order a new brace and most significantly of all, to defend his honour. Dr Drury's son Henry, who was his tutor, had called him 'a blackguard', an appellation which sent Byron into a towering rage, telling Catherine that if she did not do something to redress it, he would leave Harrow immediately – better let them take away his life than ruin his character. He also added that if she loved him she must now show it, reminding her that he was carving for himself the passage to Greatness though never to Dishonour.

Though the recipient of 'many a thundery Jobation' from Dr Drury, he was aggrieved at the idea of Drury stepping down and, with an irrational venom, opposed the appointment of a Dr Butler. When Dr Butler was appointed, Byron insisted on remaining in the same house so as to inflict torments, of which he was wondrously inventive. He circulated a broadsheet in which Butler was described as 'pomposus', a man of florid jargon, and to add piquance to the environment, he sprinkled gunpowder along the floors and tore down the iron grating over the windows, claiming that it darkened the hall.

Byron's departure was met with relief, but he did not leave as a 'finished scholar', having only come third in his grade. For his final speech day he orated King Lear's address to the storm, holding his audience so captive that news of his triumph reached Nottinghamshire. Catherine, who had not been invited, nevertheless asked Mr Hanson to send a dozen of wine and six ports to her son. Determined to avoid her, he invited himself to the Hanson household for the holiday season and further displayed his subversive spirit by firing at the cook's hat, because she had not been sufficiently beholden.

FOUR

'Four score miles' between himself and Mrs Byron, was his triumphant yodel, as the Cambridge stagecoach set out from Fetter Lane in London in October 1805. Mrs Byron and he, as he wrote to Augusta, were now totally separated, he had despaired of the futility of natural ties and sought refuge with strangers.

Of the dozen or so young bloods who enrolled at Trinity College, Byron was surely the most striking, what with his romantic aura, his strange combination of diffidence and hauteur and his 'super excellent' rooms, which Mr Hanson had been ordered to fit with furnishings, silver plate, glasses, decanters, along with four dozen of wine, port, sherry and claret. He brought his bulldog with him, a creature proving so vicious that it had to be replaced with a bear, which Byron mockingly suggested might sit for a fellowship.

Tutors and masters were soon to find that there was no checking the antics or vivaciousness of the seventeen-and-half year-old peer. Friendships burgeoned, his table was strewn with invitations and study regarded as the last of his pursuits. Those friendships that he forged at Cambridge lasted throughout his life and chief among them was John Cam Hobhouse, renamed Hobby, son of a Bristol baronet, liberal-minded, with an interest in politics and literature, penning satires in imitation of Juvenal. Another was Charles Skinner Matthews, avowed atheist and homosexual, eccentric to the point that though he was poor, he would pay a shilling in a certain coffee house in the Strand in London because he could keep his hat on. There was Scrope Davies, Byron's jovial drinking companion, 'a profane scoffer', who claimed that Byron wore paper curls in bed, which he well may have. Lastly, Douglas Kinnaird, who would eventually have the unenviable role of becoming Byron's banker.

These friendships show Byron at his most endearing. Their escapades have all the mischief, glee and daftness which Dickens would accord to Mr Pickwick and his troupe of gallants. Years later, recalling a night with Scrope at the gaming tables, before he was yet of age, Scrope, drunk, had lost everything and was being entreated by his friends to quit, except that he wouldn't. Next day, two friends with 'severe headache and empty pockets' found him in his rooms, sound asleep, without a nightcap, the chamber pot by his bedside, 'brim full of banknotes'.

His friends were ever loyal to him and, after his death, Hobhouse wrote that no man ever lived that had such devoted friends, his power of attaching people to him was magical, he was 'commanding without being over-awing, a decisiveness in his conversation and yet exceedingly free, open and unreserved'.

His first appearance in the hall at Trinity in his state robes was, as he told Hanson, quite superb. He determined to live gaily, forget the muse, which was for 'musty old sophs and fellows', forgo reading, as no one bothered to look into an author, ancient or modern; the master, as he noted, 'eats, drinks and sleeps, the fellows likewise, except that they also pun'. He was in urgent need of money, adding that he would settle for his saddle, harness and accoutrements later on. When Hanson advised some thrift, he admitted to a life of dissipation, but almost at once dashed off another letter full of umbrage towards Hanson for having charged him with that very same condition. The tone of his letters henceforth to his solicitor was peremptory and defiant. Mr Hanson was to keep Mrs Byron from ever appearing at Trinity and if that were to happen he would quit, even though rustication or expulsion might be the consequence. Most unfairly of all, he blamed that selfsame mother for his depravity, saying she had had an obligation to protect, cherish and instruct her young offspring but had failed in her duties and her perversion of temper had led to a corruption of his. He also wished it known that university was a waste for a man of his rank.

In the midst of all this dissipation, something beautiful and stirring and possibly frightening occurred. First it was the voice, silver and soaring like the skylark, the voice of a fifteen-year-old choirboy in Trinity Chapel, then the face, seen in candlelight, chiselled and beautiful. John Edleston, two years younger than Byron and an orphan of low birth, was one for whom he formed the purest and most intense passion, a mystic thread joining them both. Edleston had been recruited to Cambridge and given a stipend of one and a half shillings a term along with his board and education. In that rarefied environment, their friendship flourished, like Juno's swans, inseparable. There were glances, trysts and never a single tiresome moment between them. They went moonlighting, swam in the river below Grantchester, a secret wooded haunt that came to be called 'Byron's pool'. He showered his protégé with gifts. At the Christmas recess Edleston gave him a cornelian ring in the shape of a heart, mounted on a thin gold band, which he wore on his little finger. This 'toy of blushing hue' he celebrated in a verse, 'Pignus Amoris – The Colour of Love', in which the inexpensive jewel attests to the love of the giver, the stone, it seemed to him, emitting a tear of emotion. Neither time nor distance, he believed, could alter it, except that time, distance, caution and self-preservation brought it to a ruthless end.

Heading for London, he took lodgings with a Mrs Massingberd in Piccadilly, a room for himself and another for Fletcher, his valet. Now in the metropolis, his quarterly allowance from Chancery not payable until the New Year, he urgently needed funds. It was then and ongoingly that he put himself in the clutches of the moneylenders, the 'tribe of Levi'. 'Jew King' was the reigning moneylender of the time, whose name Byron found in a newspaper advertisement. Being a minor he wrote to his half-sister Augusta in the most 'inviolable secrecy', asking her to go as guarantor for him, adding boastfully that his property was worth one hundred times the sum he needed to raise, referring to riches that would soon be forthcoming. This surge of optimism was prompted by Mr Hanson, the perfect prototype for the dilatory and prevaricating lawyers which Dickens depicted in *Bleak House*. Without any real foundation, Mr Hanson assured him that the lawsuit to regain the Rochdale property and its lucrative collieries was progressing apace. This proved to be a figment, since it staggered on for years.

Byron asked Augusta that his request be kept secret from that 'grandee' Lord Carlisle or 'the chattering puppy, Hanson'. Augusta, wary at the thought of moneylenders, offered the few hundred pounds from her own allowance, which Byron on point of honour declined, saying he would not accept her money even if he was in danger of starvation. In her dilemma, she told Lord Carlisle and Hanson, and Byron severed relations with her, refusing to answer her pleading and contrite letters. It was Mrs Massingberd in the end who went guarantor and set Byron on the long punitive relationship with the 'sordid bloodsuckers'. Happy with his new-found, albeit indentured wealth, he wrote to his mother to say he had discharged his college bills along with debts that were left from Harrow, but that he would not be returning to Cambridge for the following term. He found it inconvenient to remain at an English university, as improvement to a man of his rank was impossible, the very idea of such a place 'ridiculous'. He intended to go abroad, France being prohibited because of England's alliance with the Bourbons against Napoleon, but Germany, the courts of Berlin, Vienna and St Petersburg were still open and he could, if necessary, be accompanied by a tutor of her choosing.

For his 'first season' in London he availed himself of many diversions, took fencing lessons from Henry Angelo and boxing lessons from John 'Gentleman' Jackson – a famous boxing champion. He was determined, as was true for his hero the hunchback Alexander Pope, that his lameness should neither blight nor curtail his prowess, claiming that the initial repugnance led to greater fierceness. Jackson, a bit of a bruiser, had great appeal for Byron, who noted his 'balustrade calf and beautifully turned but not over delicate ankle'.

But as the money ran out and he found it necessary to leave London, he warned the 'Furiosa', his mother, that he would be coming to that 'execrable kennel' at Southwell, hoping she had engaged a manservant, since his servant must attend to his horses and, moreover, that she herself cut a very indifferent figure with all those maids in her habitation.

When he did eventually return to Cambridge, the fornicating and escapading of London had not quenched his love for Edleston – on the contrary, it had deepened it.

His extravagance took an even wider radius, Edleston was showered with gifts, a hunting watch with gold chain and gold seal, and to his mother's consternation Byron acquired a carriage, along with the necessary horses, harnesses and uniformed footmen. He soon realised that Edleston was the love he could not live without and yet could not live with, as suspected sodomites were imprisoned, the crime being punishable by hanging. Contending with such looming and frightening factors, he knew that it must end, but procrastinated, being still in love. The finale came when Edleston's voice broke and being no longer an asset to the choir, he had to leave Cambridge. Byron told his cousin Elizabeth Pigot that the young man would be stationed in a mercantile house of pre-eminence in the metropolis, but as things emerged Edleston was a lowly clerk in an investment office in Lombard Street. Though his mind was a chaos of hope and sorrow, after the separation, Byron threw himself into even more daring revels, expanding his circle to include jockeys, gamblers, boxers, authors and parsons, his rooms furnished in an Ottoman style that would befit a sultan.

The bitter aftermath would occur later, when Edleston wrote to ask for help and Byron, though innately generous, bristled, causing his 'Cornelian' to write an abject and somewhat hypocritical letter saying that his only wish had been to secure Byron's patronage so that he could get a respectable occupation and not be burthensome to anyone.

Byron's comings and goings to and from Cambridge over the next three years are those of a fitful, prodigal and fugitive young Lord. He would be in some hotel or other in London, frequenting the clubs, where the dice rattled through the night, gambling on upcoming prizefighters, and consorting with prostitutes, whom he 'rescued' temporarily from the street. Lost in this abyss of sensuality, living in constant concubinage with these Marys, Corinnas or Phyllises, he sometimes had to take to his bed and undergo a course of restoration, taking Pearson's prescription for gonorrhea Virgulata, along with laudanum for the pain. The Cocoa Tree Club, a chocolate house in Piccadilly, was the popular retreat at the time, a place, as Edward Gibbon said, 'where the first men of the Kingdom in point of Fashion and Fortune assemble[d]'. Byron paints a more bibulous picture: 'We clareted and champagned till two – then supped and finished with a kind of Regency punch composed of Madeira, brandy and green tea, no real water being admitted therein.'

Jackson, as well as being his boxing master, helped in his ever-burgeoning yen for gambling, purchased a pony and pedigree greyhounds for him, along with encouraging him to bet on promising fighters. Another of his haunts was the apartment of Madame Catalani, a prima donna from the opera *Masquerade* at Covent Garden, who entertained whores, bawds and gigolos, which Byron described to Hobhouse as 'a glorious Harem'. His relationship with Caroline Cameron, a sixteen-year-old prostitute, whom he called Dahlia, was so intense that for a week or so he even considered marriage. When they went to Brighton to join his old friends Hobhouse, Scrope, Ned Long and Wedderburn Webster, Caroline was paraded on the seafront in boy's clothing, Byron introducing her to strangers as his brother Gordon. Though Byron was lame and ever conscious of it, Webster noted that he could vault 'with the agility of a harlequin'.

When the poetry 'mania' came on him, he would spin a prologue or a few satires, visiting Southwell whenever he chose, whence, by the most rigorous dieting, he had metamorphosed himself, becoming gaunt and spectral, in Hamlet guise. All his life he fretted about being overweight and in a letter to Hanson at that time, he boasted of his regime of violent exercise and fasting – 'I wear seven waistcoats and a great coat, run, and play at cricket in this Dress, till quite exhausted by excessive perspiration, use the Hip Bath daily; eat only a quarter of a pound of Butcher's Meat in twenty four hours, no Suppers or Breakfast, only one meal a day; drink no malt liquor, but a little wine, and take Physic occasionally. By these means my Ribs display skin of no great Thickness . . .'

He dabbled in love, verse, and writing plays, which he also starred in, and his cousin Elizabeth Pigot nicknamed him 'Tristam Fickle et L'Amoureuse'. It was she who observed that he did not know his own mind for more than ten minutes. His conceit was unbounded. When his tutor, the Reverend Thomas Jones, enquired if he might be returning to Cambridge, Byron's reply was categoric and condescending – 'I have other reasons for not residing at Cambridge, I dislike it . . . I have never considered it my alma mater, but rather as a nurse of no very promising appearance, on whom I have been forced against her inclinations and contrary to mine.'

The break with Edleston drew him more seriously to his poetry, perfecting and honing the several pieces which he had written over the past few years. Translations and imitations from Virgil and Anacreon were gathered together to be published in a slim volume, titled *Hours of Idleness*, in 1807. It was not, as he told Elizabeth Pigot, for the approbation of 'Citizen Mob', but for a few elite friends. It was to be published by a printer in Newark, Mr Ridge, whom Byron instructed and bullied, then sold by a Mr Crosby, a London bookseller, who would also be the butt of Byron's impetuous demands. Mr Ridge was bombarded with corrections, additions, disquisitions over the size of print, the illustrations, whether they should be of Harrow, Newstead or a portrait of Byron himself, and was latterly told to suspend all printing, as the poet had decided to give the work a new form.

Though he suffered the author's 'usual trepidations', he told his Cambridge friend William Bankes, a classicist and art collector, that he did not wish to be 'cloyed with insipid compliments', except that he did. To Elizabeth he wrote that sales were going well in the town and the watering places but sluggish with the rustics, due to provincial ignorance.

Crosby proved to be not only bookseller and friend of the printer, he was also the reviewer for the *Monthly Literary Recreations* and rhapsodised somewhat about the young and noble author, with such a degree of modesty, deciding that his beauties grew on 'the soil of genius'. In the same issue, Byron reviewed two volumes of Wordsworth's poetry, towards whom he had a political and poetic antipathy, his review confirming his stated opinion that men of the quill are sworn enemies. Wordsworth's muse, he conceded, was 'simple and flowing', but there were deformities, strong and sometimes irresistible feelings rendered with 'unexceptional sentiments'.

FIVE

Byron was now the literary swain, passing his time in some London hotel, read by duchesses, his life an annal of 'Routs, Riots, Balls and Boxing Matches, Dowagers and Demi-Reps, Cards and Crimcon [adultery], Parliamentary Discussion, Political Details, Masquerades, Mechanics . . . Wine, Women, Waxworks and Weathercocks'. He might however have been less scathing towards Wordsworth, 'the laker', had he foreseen the savagery which *Hours of Idleness* would incur. Mr Hewson Clarke, a sizar of Emmanuel College, reviewing it in *The Satirist*, wondered what could have induced 'George Gordon Lord Byron, a minor, to have favoured the world with this collection', then lampooned the Lord walking around Cambridge with his bear and heaped insults on that 'drunken harridan', Byron's mother.

But it was by a notice in the *Edinburgh Review* that Byron was 'cut to atoms'. It was the journal of the time; the reviewer, writing anonymously, was Henry Brougham, later Baron Brougham and future Lord Chancellor. Brougham excoriated him for pleading his minority, his privilege and for a mendaciousness by asking his readers to indulge his lack of talent or originality. He then went on to propose the prerequisites for a work – 'We would entreat him to believe that a certain portion of liveliness, somewhat of fancy, is necessary to constitute a poem, and that a poem in the present day, to be read, must contain at least one thought, either in a little degree different from the ideas of former writers or differently expressed.' He erroneously concluded by saying that it would be the last the world would hear of Byron.

Byron was devastated, swearing to have done with poetry for ever, his little fabric of fame among the duchesses had collapsed. In a poem, 'Stanzas to Jessy', that he had written for Edleston, he spoke of 'destiny's relentless knife' which severs lovers, and now he was to experience the relentless knives of critics, couching their spleen and venting their jealousy in lethal pedantry, for the very reason that they could never be him.

In 1808 Byron had installed himself at Newstead, a tenant Lord Grey de Ruthyn dismissed for having visited ravages upon the house, windows broken, woods further despoiled. The hares and rabbits that Lord Grey had got for his shoots had eaten all the young trees and foliage. Heedless of his debts, Byron enlisted stonemasons, carpenters, glaziers, upholsterers, so that the ancestral seat could be restored to its former glory. His tastes inclined towards the ostentatious, draperies, frills, tassels, valances, gilded four-posters, coronets, and true to his penchant for the macabre, he had skulls which had been found in the crypt, mounted on silver to be used as drinking cups.

'Time was, ere yet in these degenerate days' . . . he invited friends from Harrow and Cambridge to make merry with him, local wenches recruited as maids wearing full uniform, save for caps, which were excused. Mrs Byron was not permitted a visit, since it would not, he said, 'be proper or practical for either party'. For their evening revels the guests had to dress as monks, try their hand at a bit of amateur acting, quaff the wines and do their host's bidding. Byron remained outside it all, orchestrating these elaborate stunts, his laughter light and high and most infectious, yet curiously and tormentingly detached.

A visitor, Charles Skinner Matthews, whom Byron admired and who did not, as with many of the Cambridge circle, conceal his homosexual predilections, describes the visit in all its whimsicality to his sister. First he paints a picture of the Abbey, a fine crumbling piece of antiquity, surrounded by bleak and barren hills, its lake bordered with castellated buildings, an old kitchen, dilapidated apartments, but a 'noble room' seventy feet in length and twenty-three in breadth, for receiving. Then he guides her on an imaginary visit –

> Be mindful to go there in broad daylight, and with your eyes about you. For, should you make any blunder, should you go to the right of the hall steps, you are laid hold of by a bear; and should you go to the left, your case is still worse, for you run full against a wolf! Nor, when you have attained the door, is your danger over; for the hall being decayed, and therefore standing in need of repair, a bevy of inmates are very probably banging at one end of it with their pistols; so that if you enter without giving loud notice of your approach, you have only escaped the wolf and the bear to expire by the pistol-shots of the merry monks of Newstead ... As for our way of living, the order of the day was generally this: – for breakfast we had no set hour, but each suited his own convenience – everything remaining on the table until the whole party had done; though had one wished to breakfast at the early hour of ten, one would have been rather lucky to find any of the servants up. Our

> average hour of rising was one. I . . . was always . . . the first of the party, and was esteemed a prodigy of early rising . . . Then, for the amusements of the morning, there was reading, fencing, single-stick or shuttle-cock, in the great room; practising with pistols in the hall; walking – riding – cricket – sailing on the lake, playing with the bear, or teasing the wolf. Between seven and eight we dined; and our evening lasted . . . till one, two, or three in the morning . . . I must not omit the custom of handing round, after dinner, on the removal of the cloth, a human skull filled with burgundy. After revelling on choice viands, and the finest wines of France . . . A set of monkish dresses, which had been provided, with all the proper apparatus of crosses, beads, tonsures etcetera, often gave a variety to our appearance, and to our pursuits.

Unluckily, he fell ill in the draughty abode, then quarrelled with Hobhouse, with whom he had to walk the one hundred and thirty-five miles back to London, neither speaking, the journey taking an entire week, because of having to take shelter from the rains. Before he left, Byron had invited Skinner Matthews as a companion to Constantinople, but as he would write to his sister, it was probably 'but a wild scheme' and required 'twice thinking upon'.

SIX

Greece, for Byron, was the cradle of civilisation, yet there were less loftier reasons for his need to escape. Greece would indeed be an impetus for his future poetry, Parnassus, 'snow-clad, the "Pythian hymn" of the priestess at Delphi or Daphne's "deathless plant"'. He owed £12,000, his two ancestral seats, Newstead and Rochdale reaped next to nothing, servants went unpaid, the miners in the Lancashire coal pits threatened to revolt and his mother was obliged to lead a shiftless and stranded existence, moving from place to place and able to curb neither her son's hauteur nor his extravagances. Also there were indignant reactions to his *English Bards and Scotch Reviewers: A Satire*, a work in which he made bold and unfettered attacks on all his literary enemies, and so like Robinson Crusoe he was setting out on the 'vide vorld of vaters'.

He commissioned a miniaturist to paint portraits of all his male friends, 'heartless fellows' though they were, and was leaving England without regret. With a £2,000 loan from a Mr Birch, Hanson's partner, and bonds of over £4,000, guaranteed by his friend Scrope Davies, Byron was able to gather a motley crew for his travels. There was Joe Murray, who had been butler to the Wicked Lord, 'timber headed'

Fletcher, Byron's valet, Robert Rushton, his young comely page, on whom he had visited the 'cowpox', a Prussian who had formerly served in Persia and spoke Arabic and his friend Hobhouse, who was intending to write a book of his travels, taking with him one hundred pens and two gallons of ink.

On 2 July 1809, the packet sailed from Falmouth under the command of Captain Kidd, some of the passengers to grumble, some to spew. The inebriate Captain Kidd regaled Byron with sea stories and tales of the supernatural, one in which, asleep in his cabin, he had felt the weight of his brother's limbs, the brush of his brother's wet uniform, not knowing that that very brother had died while serving in the East Indies.

Removed from the cold climes and dark skies of England and from the constraints that though he defied them, were ever present, Byron's experience of Spain and Portugal was one of dazzlement – beauties of every description, natural and artificial, palaces and gardens rising from rocks, crags and precipices, mountains moss-embrowned, cork forests, the tender azure of the deep, chimera and fantasy amidst carnage and gore. In the aftermath of Napoleon's failed conquest of Spain and Portugal during 1808, Lisbon, their first stop, was a ravaged city, garrisoned by British and Spanish soldiers, a thousand Albion keels guarding the shore. The unclaimed dead lay with saucers on their breasts awaiting alms in the wan hope of eventual burial, and the ten thousand dogs, which the French had slaughtered before retreating, lay rotting on the streets. Beauty and carnage conjoined, each sight seeping into his unconscious as he accrued the startling material for his poetry.

The experiences of the next two years of travel would yield

not just eggs and oranges and fleas and hard beds and stinking latrines and 'fooleries' with boys and young women, it would also provide the shimmering background for his poem *Childe Harold*, initially called *Childe Burun*, the lowly lay of a youth, darkly disconsolate, who had spent his time 'in riot most uncouth', drugged with pleasures, longing betimes for woe, and in imitation of Dante's penitents journeying to the Underworld to witness the straits of the departed.

Such a proliferation of sights and sounds, encounters with generals and admirals, princes and pashas, a variety of conjugal excitements, the classical beauty of Greece, the natural beauty of Albania, dangers and hazards in remote places without a name, changed Byron both as a man and as an artist. Yet something remained, the melancholy that could be routed out and the wounds of childhood. On a much later journey, exiled from England in disgrace in 1814, he remarked in his 'Alpine Journal', written for Augusta, that the woods of withered trees, their trunks stripped and barkless, their branches lifeless, reminded him of himself and of his family. For all his gaiety and legendary colloquy, Byron was obsessed with the idea of a withering, recalling more than once Swift's remark of 'dying at the top', signifying the loss of reason, a dread he shared with the Mad Dean.

His time abroad would also yield a crop of imperious letters to his solicitor Hanson, who was not sending remittances fast enough, because Byron had determined to live like a potentate.

'I should have joined the army, but we have no time to lose before we get up the Mediterranean and Archipelago', he wrote to his mother, masking the fact that political idealism does not tally with the horror of war. As he saw it, there were no winners, all were eventual victims and this conviction would be tellingly rendered both in *Childe Harold* and *Don Juan*, the foe, the victim and the fond ally fighting for all but fighting in vain, corpses to feed the ravens and fertilise the fields.

His letters were also filled with the observations and playfulness of a young man adapting himself to the habits of another country – 'I loves oranges, and talks bad Latin to the monks . . . and I goes into society (with my pocket pistols), and I swims in the Tagus . . . and I rides on an ass or a mule, and swears Portuguese, and have got a diarrhoea and bites from the mosquitoes,' he wrote to his friend Francis Hodgson. Hobhouse and he, being of such contrasting dispositions, saw things differently, Hobhouse disgusted by lasciviousness and Byron enthralled by it. For Hobhouse, the women, nasty and frightful, were 'the ugliest race of animals', whereas for Byron, the Portuguese and Spanish belles, with their glossy black hair and large black eyes, their gift of intrigue, were irresistible, replacing the 'Lancashire witches' in his affections.

So the party of men, Rushton, Fletcher, old Joe Murray, Hobby and Byron, travelled and bickered, searched for rooms in inns and in the headquarters of the defeated royalist militia. Byron and Hobhouse would leave their cards with various ambassadors and consuls, sometimes to no avail, and arriving in Seville they were obliged to take lodgings with the two unmarried Beltram sisters. They went 'supperless and dinnerless' as Hobhouse noted and even worse, were crammed into one little bedroom, not at all the salubrious setting that Byron would have liked. But very soon the charms of the sisters compensated, especially Donna Josepha, the elder, who became his 'preceptress' in love, a passion they furthered with the aid of a dictionary.

In the Governor's box at a bullfight in Cadiz, Byron was both captivated and repelled, the savagery, the ceremony, the blood-lust of the spectators, more shocking than the disembowelling of man or beast, the effect on him so profound that he devoted eleven stanzas of *Childe Harold* to this Sabbath death. In the Cathedral he vented his wonted repugnance for art, hating the works of Velázquez and Murillo, blaspheming all art, unless it reminded him of something, and feeling as if he might spit on the representations of saints. But Donna Josepha had furnished him with sweet moments and sweet memories and on his departure for Cadiz, she had cut off a lock of her hair, three feet in length, which he sent to his mother to be 'retained' until he returned home, though perversely vowing that he would never return to England again.

His ambiguity about his native land revealed itself at every twist and turn and standing on the quayside with Hobby, witnessing the celebratory landing of Sir Arthur Wellesley, the future Lord Wellington, Byron railed at the sight of Wellesley charioteering over the French flag, because Napoleon was and would remain Byron's god. He held with Charles Fox's creed that the fall of the Bastille was the greatest and best event in the history of the world.

Poised for adventures in the East and the Socratic pleasures, intending to 'cull as many hyacinths as possible', he sent Joe Murray home, along with Rushton, asking his mother to show the lad kindness, saying he would have taken him but that young boys were not safe among the Turks.

On the packet *Townshend* to Malta in August, Byron caught

the attentions of John Galt, a Scotsman who having failed as entrepreneur and smuggler, had taken up the trade of literature and became one of the many who attached themselves to Byron, studied his every mood and wrote down his Quixotic conversation in order to preserve him in their own distinctive aspic. 'Boswellised' as Byron would call it, though none had Boswell's humour, humanity or genius. Seeing Byron embarking, Galt noticed that His Lordship manifested more aristocracy than befitted his years or the occasion. His dress was that of a metropolitan beau, with its own peculiarity of style, the physiognomy prepossessing and intelligent but with a terrible scowl. Byron, the embodiment of a poet, stood alone at the ship's rails, leaned on the mizzen shrouds, seeming to study the gloomy rocks in the distance. Then after three days as his humour bettered he provided pistols, encouraging his fellow passengers and Galt to shoot at bottle tops as he uncorked vast quantities of champagne 'in the finest condition'.

As his horizons widened, so did his sense of entitlement. Preparing for an audience with the King of Sardinia, he purchased a most superb uniform of court dress, but had to settle for the sight of the royal family in a box at the opera, to which the British Minister, a Mr Hill, had brought him. Again, before arriving at Malta, he had a message sent to the Governor, Sir Alexander Ball, believing that due to his rank he would be welcomed by a royal salute of guns. As the other passengers disembarked, Hobby and Byron waited on board and by dusk, when no such honour was forthcoming, they had to be rowed to the port, somewhat dejected and crestfallen.

They were eventually received by the Governor, who arranged lodgings for them in a house belonging to a Dr

Moncrieff, and were soon welcomed as gallants in English social circles. Determined to have some knowledge of Arabic for their ongoing journey, Byron bought an Arabic grammar book and engaged a tutor to give him lessons, his studies, however, halted by the emergence of 'absurd womankind'. A ravishing beauty with translucent skin, golden hair and brilliant blue eyes, such was his new-found 'Calypso' in the person of the 26-year-old Mrs Constance Smith. Daughter of an Austrian baron, 'select' friend of the Queen of Naples and somewhat tepid wife of John Spencer Smith, Constance was a woman 'touched with adventure' and her story could easily have emanated from the pen of Lord Byron. In 1806 she had been arrested by the Napoleonic government in Venice and while being conveyed under heavy guard to a prison at Valenciennes in France, she was dramatically rescued by a Sicilian marquis who was in love with her and who had conceived this daredevil ingenious scheme. They travelled incognito from inn to inn, Constance in the disguise of a page boy, midnight escapades through windows, until finally the marquis secured a boat to ferry her across Lake Garda and thereafter to her family in Graz. Byron and she became inseparable and writing to his mother, towards whom he had become more cordial, he extolled the 'extraordinary' and 'eccentric' Constance. They were, he believed, on the brink of elopement to the Friuli Mountains, north of Venice, except that Constance was expected, as mother of two, to join her husband in England. Before their parting, Constance had relieved him of his large yellow diamond ring. Before setting sail, Byron challenged a Captain Cary to a duel, believing he had impeached his inamorata's honour, but luckily for him, Hobhouse had huddled him onto a brig-of-war bound for Patras in Greece. Constance was poeticised as 'Sweet Florence' and in *Childe Harold* would be accorded the enchantments of 'Calypso', but after three weeks the 'everlasting passion' had faded, the spell was broken and Byron's attachments would be transferred to beautiful young men 'with all the Turkish vices'.

Byron's love at that time, whether towards young men or women, was always high-flown, bathed in romantic, glowing and sometimes furtive light and always ending in ennui with his departure towards new latitudes and new conquests.

Albania, 'rugged nurse of savage men', was part of the Ottoman Empire and within sight of Italy, but as Gibbon had said was 'as unknown as the interior of America'. Byron, Hobhouse, Fletcher, 'the reverse of valiant', and Albanian soldiers armed with sabres and long guns set out with their equipment of four leather trunks, three smaller trunks, a canteen, three beds and bedding, two bed-heads, on horse-back, over rugged land, where the beauties of nature and the savageries of man starkly contrasted, domes, minarets, orange and lemon groves, mutilated bodies and roasted heads left hanging as a warning to other offenders.

Ali Pasha, a ruthless Turkish vizier, governed Albania, Epirus, Macedonia and parts of Greece as far south as the Gulf of Corinth and was said to have more power than the Sultan. For his redoubtable conquests, he had been chris-tened 'Mahometan Napoleon' and Napoleon had offered to make him King of Epirus, except that friendship with the English suited his political ambitions better. Hearing that an Englishman of rank, that is to say Byron, was in his dominions, Ali Pasha left orders with his commandant in the city of Jannina that the party be treated with hospitality, he at that very time engaged in *une petite guerre* with another warlord, Ibrahim Pasha, whom he had driven into a fortress in Berat.

To Byron the landscape recalled the Highlands of his childhood, the castles like those Sir Walter Scott had depicted, the very mountains seemed Caledonian, the Albanians in kilts, the strut of their cloaks, the shimmer of their daggers, all reminiscent of Highland warriors. Albania was a mixture of races, Albanians in their gold-worked cloaks and crimson jackets, Tartars with high caps, Turks in their vast pelisses and turbans and such were the arcane laws of loyalty or disloyalty that a throat could be slit at the slightest affront. The young women whom Byron thought the most beautiful he had ever seen were 'beasts of burthen', ploughing, digging and levelling the highways broken down by torrential rains.

His letters home were jaunty, asking for news of deaths, defeats, capital crimes and misfortunes of his friends. His mother learnt that if he married it would be with a sultana who had half a score of cities as a dowry.

In full 'magnifique' Albanian uniform, with a silver sabre, he was received at Ali Pasha's court in Tepelene, a room paved with marble, a fountain playing in the centre, scarlet ottomans all around and a physician to conduct the colloquy in Latin. His Highness the Pasha, aged about sixty, was a short fat man with a long white beard, with a surprising mildness of manner, whose own head would one day be on a stake in Constantinople. He was immediately drawn to the young and beautiful Lord, 'a pretty stripling', whose small ears and very white hands bespoke the true rank of nobility. At first he enquired after Byron's health, then respects were paid to Byron's mother, then to Byron's singular beauty, followed by a request that Byron would regard him as 'Father' for as long as he remained in the Empire and pay a visit to him at night when he would be at his leisure.

Byron and Hobhouse were assigned quarters in the palace, their every necessity gratis, and from Ali Pasha twenty times a day Byron was coaxed with gifts of sherbet, almonds and sweetmeats. In their honour each evening a feast was prepared, four fires blazed in the courtyard for kids and sheep to be roasted, black slaves, eunuchs and hundreds of soldiers in attendance, horses caparisoned and ready for action, couriers constantly entering and leaving with dispatches, the kettle drums beaten, boys calling the hour from the minaret of the mosque, whirling dervishes, and the boastful recital of great and barbarous deeds.

After a one-month stay, it was time for the travellers to take their leave and on a galliot with a crew of forty, provided by Ali Pasha, they set out but were almost shipwrecked on the way to Greece, the Turks being no great navigators. Byron, revelling in danger, described it graphically to his mother –

> Two days ago I was nearly lost in a Turkish ship of war owing to the ignorance of the captain and crew . . . Fletcher yelled after his wife, the Greeks called on all the saints, the Mussulmans on Alla; the captain burst into tears and ran below deck, telling us to call on God; the sails were split, the main-yard shivered, the wind blowing fresh, the night setting in, and all our chance was to make Corfu, which is in possession of the French, or (as Fletcher pathetically termed it) a watery grave. I did what I could to console Fletcher, but finding him incorrigible, wrapped myself up in my Albanian capote, and lay down on deck to wait the worst.

They escaped drowning only because the captain allowed the few Greek sailors on board to manage the ship and make anchorage on the rocky coast of Suli in northern Greece.

SEVEN

'Fair Greece! sad relic of departed worth! . . . Who now shall lead thy scattered children forth . . . ?' Byron's plans were to spend a year in Athens to study modern Greek and then to set out for Asia. Travelling by land, through robber-infested passes, they arrived at Missolonghi, a flat marshy promontory with a few fishermen's huts built on stakes in the water, where no Sphinx was there to foretell that some fifteen years later it would become the last fateful domicile of Lord Byron.

At the ancient site of what was left of Delphi, the aspiring men of letters, Hobhouse and Byron scratched their names on a broken column. At the foot of Parnassus, seeing a flight of eagles, which Hobhouse insisted were vultures, Byron took it as an auspicious sign from the god Apollo and there and then composed a stanza for *Childe Harold*.

On Christmas Day in 1809 Byron had his first view of the Plain of Athens, Hymettus, the Aegean, the Acropolis 'burst upon the eye at once' and a more glorious sight he had never seen. They took rooms in the house of Tarsia, widow of a Greek who had been a British vice-consul and mother of three beautiful daughters, all under fifteen, the 'Divinities', who with their red Albanian skullcaps and yellow slippers, behaved with infinite courtesy when they served at the frugal table. Like that other great specialist of the female form, Gustave Flaubert, whose libidinous genius was quickened when he went to Egypt, Byron noted every feature and gesture of the Divinities; in the evening doing needlework or playing the tambourine, they removed their slippers and tantalisingly gathered their limbs under their clothing on the divan.

'Damn description' he would say, but his bulletins to his friends and to his mother, swift and uncluttered, are marvels of observation, the waves of the Aegean sapphire and gold, the beauty of Illyria, the bogs of Boeotia, places without names, rivers not laid down in maps, discoveries to fuel his zest for adventure. The Troad, the plains of Troy, he described at first as a fine field where a good sportsman and an ingenious scholar could exercise feet and faculties. He went each day and sat on the tomb of Patroclus and read Book Eight of Pope's translation of the *Iliad*, praising Pope's genius and berating those coxcombs who had 'topographised and typographised King Priam's dominion in three days', upstarts who questioned the siege of Troy, obliterating the greatness of Achilles, Ajax and Antilochus.

Byron's curiosity was inexhaustible and his mind encyclopaedic. Julius Caesar wore a wreath of laurels to hide his baldness and not because he was a conqueror and Prometheus's fire was a fire of the mind. In less classical mode, he noted that the Turks had no foreskins, that sodomy and smoking were the main vices and that St Paul need not have bothered with his epistles at Ephesus, as the church he preached in was converted to a mosque.

Heroic musings were mingled with regret at the loss of the golden age of Athens. The narrow streets were crammed and squalid, Turks, Greeks and Albanians jostling for a foothold and everywhere, ruins, 'a nation's sepulchre' as he put it, the haunts of the gods no longer revered as shrines. At the Acropolis he saw and rued the crumbling pediments, columns defaced by elements, defaced by time, by conquest and by looters, ruins that mirrored the ruin within himself and the wounds that would magnify and that he sought to repress through love, through poetry and through action. He lashed out against the paltry and grasping antiquarians, filling their vessels with valuable and massy relics and his particular wrath was reserved for Lord Elgin, whose dastardly devastation of the Parthenon was a rape, marbles taken and dispatched to England ostensibly to enlighten aspiring architects and sculptors. In *The Curse of Minerva*, published in 1812, the goddess not only curses Lord Elgin but curses those he will sire and Byron likens the brazen robbery to the ravages of Turk or Goth. The honour of England, as he said, would never be advanced by the plunder of Attica.

Before sailing east for Constantinople in April 1810, Byron had 'hot from the anvil' completed the first draft of *Childe Harold*, which Hobhouse dismissed as having too much exaggeration and declamation. Byron put it in his travelling trunk and decided to seek glory otherwise. When the frigate *Salsette* anchored at the strait of the Dardanelles, he and Lieutenant Eakenhead swam the broad Hellespont, from Sestos to Abydos, a feat of which he was more proud than he could possibly be over any other glory, political, poetical or rhetorical. He had placed himself among the ranks of the mythic Greek hero Leander, who as Ovid said, 'at the command of love', swam each night to visit his love, the priestess Hero, in her tower at Sestos. Byron, in less mythic mode, decided that Leander's conjugal powers would have been extremely depleted by the swim.

As they approached Constantinople in windy weather,

Hobhouse described the 'vast capital rising from the forests of cypresses and overtopped with innumerable domes and slender spires', whereas Byron was struck by the gloom of the Seraglio walls that protected the empire of the 'Eastern Caesars'. A proliferation of new, startling sights and sounds, streets bustling with thieves, jesters, trafficking women, teeming humanity, splendid things and shocking things, the dogs lapping up the blood of the slain, yet Byron shirking from nothing because as a poet his manifesto was that he would write 'from the fullness of [his] mind, from passion, from impulse, from many motives, but never for the sweet voice'.

In the city in his gold-embroidered scarlet dress and feathered cocked hat he attracted attention, his delicate features however suggesting a feminine appearance and even Sultan Mahmoud II, who received him on his throne in yellow satin, his turban alive with diamonds, was convinced that the English Lord was 'a woman in man's clothes'.

While in Constantinople, Byron learnt three essential Turkish words – 'pimp', 'bread' and 'water'. Hobhouse meanwhile was preparing to go home at his father's most insistent summoning. In July 1810, the *Salsette* pulled in to the harbour of Keos in Greece and the two friends parted, Hobhouse describing it as 'tearful' as they divided a nosegay of flowers, whereas Byron rejoiced that the year of purgatory with Hobhouse was over. Yet before long he was resuming his affectionate tone in letters – 'After all I do love thee, Hobby, thou hast so many good qualities and so many bad ones.'

Byron returned to Athens and took lodgings in the fourth-century Capuchin monastery at the foot of the Acropolis, in the company of boys and men. He had wearied of the daughters and maids of Athens, because their mothers had tried to dragoon him into marriage.

Hymettus before him, Acropolis behind him, fed on woodcock and red mullet, drinking wine with the monks, he was blissfully happy, his days 'a riot of one kind or another from noon till night'. In this Paradise of men and boys, he selected one of the 'sylphs', fifteen-year-old Nicolo Giraud, a pupil at the monastery, to be his pet, and writing to Skinner Matthews, he said he intended to relieve the boy of his very last inhibition.

As was true for all his deeds, Byron was credited or discredited with either acts of courage or blatant dissipation. One evening, on his ride back to the city from the woods, he saw that a girl sewn into a sack was about to be cast into the sea by the Turkish police for her crime of illicit love. With threats and ultimately with a bribe, Byron persuaded them to give up the girl and later that night he had her shipped in secrecy to Thebes. Rumours of this chivalrous rescue circulated in Athens among the English set. It was also insinuated that Byron had been the girl's lover and hence the cause of her near-execution, something he was uncustomarily reticent about, except that the incident and the terror it instilled in him remained 'icy even to recollect', the feelings re-rendered in a poem, *The Giaour*, written in 1813.

The 35-year-old Lady Hester Stanhope, another indefatigable English traveller, besotted by the East, whom Hobhouse had described as a 'violent peremptory person', happened to be in Athens at that time, with her younger lover Michael Bruce. From her launch as she arrived in Athens, she sighted Byron diving at Piraeus harbour, where he swam each day, and while her lover would fall under Byron's spell, Lady Hester did not. Byron was somewhat hesitant in her company, ever nervous as he said of 'that dangerous thing a female wit' and determined not to 'argufy' with her. She thought him a poseur. To her physician Dr Meryon, who travelled with her, she said that Byron '[was] all avarice and capriciousness, everything he [said] and [did had] an ulterior motive'. Hearing of the rescue of the girl, Lady Hester said Byron wanted to prove himself to be 'a sort of Don Quixote'. Contrary to all the plaudits about his beauty, Lady Hester remarked on the vice in his looks, 'his eyes set too close together and a contracted brow'. This would contrast glaringly with another description of Byron from the surgeon Dr Forrester, of the sloop *Alacrity*, who would say, years later, that the expressive furrows that streaked Byron's forehead 'disappeared with the fleeting rapidity of the Aurora Borealis'. Lady Hester mimicked Byron for her English friends, his habit of drawing a little curl over his forehead and speaking Romaic, modern Greek, to his servants with silly affectation.

So even as Byron was caught up in these several adventures, the elite circles in London were hearing glimmerings of him. His letters to his mother and Mr Hanson were increasingly summonses for remittances, yet his letters to Hobhouse and Scrope Davies brimmed with accounts of coitus, the sylphs, as he called them, 'vastly happy and childish'. Nicolo, at 'his own most pressing solicitation', followed Byron everywhere and as he said to Hobhouse, it was *padrone* and *amico* and puppy-like sexual cavorts. Tom Moore, however, described these liaisons as 'brotherly'.

For Byron Greece was 'the Dome of Thought, the Palace of the Soul'. He loved the mountains, the blue Aegean and its isles, the stones, the fallen columns, skies redolent of heaven and everywhere the spectre of lost valour. It was also, he believed, the nation which made him a poet. Kindled in him then, at the age of twenty-two, was the necessity for Greek independence, Greece betrayed or pawned by Russians, French and English, needing but a convoy of arms, to rise up against the Ottoman tyrant.

If he could receive 'cash and comfortable news' he would not trouble 'the foggy island' of England again. The 'comfortable news' came as a summons from Scrope Davies, the loans he had guaranteed in 1809 had gone unpaid, as had the interest on them, for which Scrope was responsible.

'I cannot sleep and much fear madness,' Scrope wrote, adding that he was being hounded by annuitants and creditors and was subject to arrest day after day. Byron had written to him in the intervening time, the letters a miscellany of ramblings, sojourns, lubricities in bathhouses, ending with the insouciant hope that Scrope was 'in good plight', and that his agents had released him of any responsibility. Except that they hadn't. His solicitor, Mr Hanson, had not communicated with him for over a year, leaving him to assume, in his make-believe fantasia regarding money, that Rochdale had been sold, that the lands in Norfolk had been sold, that debts were paid and that he was an affluent young man. It was not until Scrope wrote to say 'Nothing but your return can relieve me' that Byron, albeit lurchingly, realised that he must go home. He brought Nicolo Giraud with him to Malta. There he met, at her instigation, Mrs Constance Smith, who was holding him to a sacred promise, but the flame was quenched and moreover he was suffering from tertian fever, haemorrhoids and syphilis, having been 'clapped' as many of the English fraternity in Athens were, from Greek and Turkish women. Having enrolled Nicolo in a Jesuit school, in May 1811 Byron set out for England consumed with disgust and disenchantment, so that neither maid nor youth could delight him any longer.

In his journal he set down his mordant feelings –

> At twenty three the best of life is over and its bitters double. I have seen mankind in various Countries and find them equally despicable, if anything the Balance is rather in favour of the Turks. 3dly I am sick at heart . . . 4thly A man who is lame of one leg is in a state of bodily inferiority, which increases with years and must render his old age more peevish & intolerable. Besides, in another existence I expect to have *two* if not *four* legs by way of compensation. 5thly I grow selfish and misanthropical. 6thly My affairs at home and abroad are gloomy enough. 7thly I have outlived all my appetites and most of my vanities aye even the vanity of authorship.

The journey on the frigate *Volage*, from Malta to England, took six weeks, giving Byron ample time to recall the licentiousness and wonders of his travels, the Turkish baths, 'those marble paradises of sherbet and sodomy', and to contemplate his very precarious future. He must go to Notts to raise rents, to Lancs to sell collieries, back to London to settle debts and then board a cargo ship for anywhere. In a bristling letter to his mother he resumed his peremptory tone –

> You will be good enough to get my apartments ready at Newstead; but don't . . . consider me in any other light than as a visiter. I must only inform you that for a long time I have been restricted to an entire vegetable diet, neither fish nor flesh . . . so I expect a powerful stock of potatoes, greens, and biscuit; I drink no wine. I have two servants, middle-aged men, and both Greeks . . . I don't suppose I shall be much pestered with visiters; but if I am,

> you must receive them, for I am determined to have nobody breaking in upon my retirement: you know that I never was fond of society, and I am less so than before. I have brought you a shawl, and a quantity of attar of roses.

A letter to Francis Hodgson gives a more candid picture of his despair – 'I am returning home without a hope, and almost without a desire' he wrote on that long introspective voyage home. With him were two Greek servants, his paraphernalia consisting of four ancient Athenian skulls, a phial of Attic hemlock and four live tortoises. On 14 July 1811 the frigate docked at Sheerness in the Thames Estuary on the Isle of Sheppey, two years after his departure. He did not hurry to Newstead or Rochdale to settle his 'irreparable affairs', but installed himself at Reddish's Hotel in St James's Street. His first and most pressing imperative was a trip to the money-lenders, though his former landlady, Mrs Massingberd, could no longer go guarantor for him, her own finances being catastrophic. Old friends rejoiced at his homecoming, Hodgson burst into appalling verse – 'Return my Byron to Britannia's fair' – Scrope Davies arrived 'with a new set of jokes' and Byron, on borrowed money, set out for Kent to visit Hobhouse, who at his father's insistence had joined the militia and was now Captain Hobhouse, about to be dispatched to Ireland with his regiment, to keep the precarious peace.

Regardless of his straits, Byron resumed his opulent ways, ordered a vis-à-vis, which he presently had to exchange for a carriage belonging to another Cambridge friend, the bold Sir Wedderburn Webster. Despite his lifelong and averred admiration for Napoleon and his dislike of the Duke of Wellington, he blithely informed his solicitor Mr Hanson that he might join the campaign in Spain. He spoke of his own lackadaisical quality at that time, but it could be more accurately described as a paralysing indecision. Money being the magnet, as he said in a letter to his sister Augusta, Hanson was also being instructed to squeeze remittances from the collieries at Rochdale and secure copyhold rights for the estates in Norfolk.

In his trunk there were two works, which he had penned abroad, the first, a satire, *Hints from Horace*, for which he had high hopes, and the second, Cantos One and Two of a long poetic narrative in Spenserian measure, which was called *Childe Harold's Pilgrimage*, having been previously named *Childe Burun's Pilgrimage*. These he entrusted to a kinsman by marriage soon to become his self-appointed agent, Reverend Robert Charles Dallas, to get his opinion of them. Dallas thought the satire insipid, but having read *Childe Harold* and shown it to Walter Wright, who had been Consul-General of the Ionian Islands, they decided that Byron had 'struck a vein of gold'. The mythologising and legendising of a young poet whose experiences, though manifold, still left him alone in the world, had a whiff of greatness and originality. Those scenes in the East of palaces and gardens and shipwrecks and decapitated bodies and slave women and thwarted love and wine bouts and Ottomans and Mussulmans had been put to thrilling use by the young Lord. For his ingratiating report Dallas was handed the copyright of the poem as a gift and so set about finding a publisher.

On 23 July, intending to travel north with Hanson to visit the beleaguered coalfields, he sent a cryptic letter to his mother, giving her timely notice of his brief visit, adding that she may in future consider Newstead as her house and not his. He did not allude to the bailiffs that were installed in the

Abbey or the numerous demands from creditors that had been pinned on the front door, then covered over with brown paper by the ingenious Joe Murray. Away from Catherine, his letters were friendly, often confiding, though not of course alluding to the sherbet and sodomy debauches. But now that he was about to meet with her again the old residual anger and subsequent hauteur resurfaced. It was in Athens, to his friend the Marquis of Sligo, that he had described the final scene with Mrs Byron before he left England, she succumbing to one of her 'fits' willing that he might prove as ill-formed in mind as he was in body.

Poor Mrs Byron, as Tom Moore put it in his biography of Byron, was a woman 'whose excessive corpulence rendered her at all times, rather a perilous subject for illness' and so it was that she was indisposed while Byron lingered in London, and with a sad prescience she said to her maid, 'If I should be dead before Byron comes down, what a strange thing it would be.' That is exactly what happened. On 1 August he got a letter from the local physician to say her condition was worsening and that he was apprehensive for 'the Event'. Byron, cash-strapped once again, went to Hanson to borrow money and Hanson not being in his office, Mrs Hanson had to lend him £40 for the journey. It was on his way to Newstead at a coaching inn that Robert Rushton arrived on horseback to tell him that his mother had died. The servants at the Abbey were overcome with grief and soon the Prodigal Son would sink into that same state of bathos and remorse.

There were different reports as to what Catherine had died from, obesity, dropsy, drunkenness, and one claim that she had died in a fit of rage upon receiving an upholsterer's bill for £1,600, money owed for furnishings that Byron had ordered before his departure to the Levant. It was only when he saw the corpse that Byron broke down. He sat beside her all night in the dark and could be heard calling out, 'Oh Mrs By, I had but one friend in the world.' Too stricken to accompany the hearse to Hucknall Torkard next day, he watched the carriage and the pallbearers go down the drive and then called to Rushton to get his boxing gloves and without speaking, jabbed and punched with a violence he had not hitherto shown, then threw down his gloves and left the room. Her faults would be washed away as she became his amiable Mama, he at three and twenty left alone and no one with whom to 'retrace the laughing part of life'.

His grief was compounded by news of other deaths. Hobhouse informed him by letter that their friend Skinner Matthews had drowned in canal water, enmeshed in a bed of weeds in the Cam River in Cambridge, leaving not a scrap of paper to enlighten his friends as to why he had taken his own life. Byron was devastated, believing some curse hung over him, and scarcely able to live with his feelings he wrote to Scrope Davies, 'Come to me, Scrope, I am almost desolate.'

Not too long after, he received a letter from Ann Edleston to say that her brother John had died of consumption in May. At once Edleston was enshrined in a poem and given the name Thyrza to disguise his sex –

Yet did I love thee to the last
As fervently as thou,
Who didst not change through all the past,
And canst not alter now.

The poem would be added to *Childe Harold*, but not before Dallas was informed that it was addressed to no particular person. Poetry aside, he felt remorse and disgust at not having spared 'a better being'.

EIGHT

Certain publishers, whom Dallas had approached, had rejected *Childe Harold* on grounds of indecency and also because of Byron's wayward attacks on writers in the earlier satire, *English Bards and Scotch Reviewers*, published in March 1809. But Mr John Murray, publisher and bookseller of 32 Fleet Street, 'who ranked high among the brethren of the trade', responded favourably. He was the publisher of Walter Scott, Robert Southey, the critic William Gifford and Jane Austen, who by being a woman, mattered less in that masculine constellation. *Childe Harold*, begun in Jannina in Albania in 1809 and completed at Smyrna in 1810, with its exotic and ghastly descriptions happened to suit the prevailing taste for 'strong excitement'.

Mr John Murray's letter of acceptance to Byron was so complimentary that Byron said it was not usual, as Dr Johnson had noted, 'to hear the truth from one's bookseller'. Yet Byron baulked. Dallas tells us he had extreme repugnance about being published at all, while at the same time he was craving immortality. In the end he agreed, emphasising the fact that *Childe Harold* must not be confused with him.

In youthful noblesse Byron took no money for the work, the profits being shared equally between Dallas and John

Murray, who had paid for the printing and publication. And so began a relationship unique between author and publisher, as intriguing as any marriage, but more erudite; flattery, disquiet and rebuttal, as they praised, scolded and jabbed, threats of defection from Byron followed by sudden reconciliation, a devious dance of dependence and independence, charted vividly in their rum exchange of letters. Byron would allude to the natural antipathy between bookseller and author, the 'ferine nature' of the bookseller always breaking forth, forgetting to mention his own violent nature. Murray would come to know Byron the Classicist, Byron the Jester, Byron the Buffoon, Byron the Bulldog, Byron the Stoic, Byron the Lover and Poet and increasingly, Byron the lover of 'lucre'.

Murray guessed that Cantos One and Two would indeed strike an immediate chord, the young hero sick 'with the fullness of satiety' and rejecting all thought or hope of redemption was bound to have an appeal in Regency England, except that there were problems. He was appealing to Dallas to persuade Byron to remove or at least 'soften' some of the more dangerous stanzas and to temper his outrageous religious sentiments, which were bound to deprive Mr Murray of customers 'among the orthodox'. Byron parried. He had no time for religion, said it was rife with rival villainous sects 'tearing each other to pieces for the love of the Lord and hatred of each other'. Murray especially objected to unpatriotic passages concerning the war in Spain and Portugal, when Byron was critical of the sovereign allies, sentiments which certainly did not harmonise with the general, prevalent feeling in England. Byron was intransigent, being too sincere for recantation, adding that with regard to the political content, he could alter nothing and anyhow had high authority for his 'errors on that point', because the *Aeneid* was a political poem and written for a political purpose. Depicting battles and barbarities from ancient times, it reflected the spirit of his own time, England at war, even as Regency London was hellbent on banquet and profligacy. He would however oblige, tag on some more rhymes or stanzas, write an introductory stanza if the poem opened too abruptly, and these offerings he brought in person to Mr Murray's office, fencing at the bookshelves, jesting as he tried to anticipate Murray's opinion, quoting Congreve with a warning – 'If you put me in a phrenzy I will never call you Jack again.'

NINE

'The poet yields to the orator' Byron announced to Dallas as he prepared for his maiden speech in the House of Lords. He chose to speak for the Whig opposition against the Tory Framework Bill. In 1811 the weavers of Nottingham had rioted because the manufacturers had introduced new machinery for the making of gloves and stockings, so that one man could take the place of seven. The weavers reacted by breaking the new machines, militia regiments were sent to quell them and a commission appointed to try them and possibly sentence them to hanging. Byron deferred to Lord Holland, leader of the Whig Party, nephew and protégé of Charles James Fox, saying his motive for speaking was the palpable injustice and efficiency of the Tory law, adding that his speech would be brief.

So in February 1812, he was plunged into all that Gothic splendour, peers in their scarlet and ermine robes bristling to outdo one another in wit and invective, innately suspicious of a newcomer. It is hardly surprising that Byron would be nervous and Dallas tells us that he wrote out his entire speech and then memorised it 'like a Harrow oration'. His voice normally sweet and melodious became unnatural as he declaimed to the assembled House the injustice and the inequity of the

Bill, insisting it was not punishment those starving workers deserved, but compassion and bread for their children. 'Will you erect a gibbet in every field, and hang up men like scarecrows?' he asked. He challenged them by asking if a human life was valued at less than the price of a stocking frame, and Lord Eldon the Lord Chancellor was put very much out of humour by such audaciousness. He quoted passages from Cobbett, his sentences having the construction of Edmund Burke's, a little theatrical as he later conceded, but afterwards he was very elated by compliments from his own party and the opposition. That evening, in a gathering at Lord Holland's, his host praised him fulsomely, but in his memoirs Holland would say that Byron's speech, full of fancy, wit and invective, 'was not exempt from affectation, not well balanced, not well reasoned and not suited to the common notion of political eloquence'.

It mattered not. Byron was launched. Dallas saw the speech as the best advertisement for *Childe Harold* and Murray delayed the publication for a few days in March, the better to whet the appetite of a curious elite. Sheets of the poem were dispatched to influential people and advertisements in the *Courier* and *Morning Chronicle* titillated them with what was to come. The first edition of five hundred copies was sold out in three days as Murray hastened to print a second smaller edition at half the price. Byron's 'reign' would last through spring and summer, he, the only topic of conversation, men jealous of him and women 'stark mad' over him, besieging him with letters, both openly and clandestinely, enough, as he boasted, to fill a volume. A shop window carried a copy of *Childe Harold*, which had been specially bound for Princess Charlotte, the daughter of the Prince Regent.

Praise was unanimous. Tom Moore described Byron as as

much 'the child of the revolution, in poesy, as another great man of the age, Napoleon, was in statesmanship and warfare'. Critics who had formerly attacked his youthful and precocious verses were won over by the strength, vibrancy and startling genius of the new work. Dallas remarked on Byron's temper being 'soothed', but for Byron, only twenty-four and fame unfurling so rapidly, there were other hidden consequences, a duality, a self-deluding grandeur, a necessity to fall in love with some heiress despite his homosexual proclivities, and above all, not to be toppled from his throne.

Carriages bearing invitations from the nobility thronged the street of his lodgings in St James's and the lame poet with the features of Adonis was thrust upon the world.

And so he was welcomed into the drawing rooms of the Whig aristocracy, Holland House, Melbourne House, Devonshire House, the recherché society, which as Leslie Marchand wrote in his massive biography of Byron, were places 'where irregularities of conduct were the prerogatives of an uninhibited upper class'. In a city of one million inhabitants, Byron met only with the privileged, apart from his servants and his firelighter, the withered Mrs Mule. The world of poverty, destitution, oppression, lawlessness and riots, that of thieves, pedlars, harlots and drunks, the lame and indigent, the 'swinish multitude' who thronged to Tyburn to see the executions did not have a place in Byron's works. The East in all its mystery, was the mainspring for his creative energies.

Though more at home in the company and bantering of intellectual men, Byron was swamped by women, all seeing him as the archetype of Childe Harold, despite his every camouflage not to be. There was something cold and fastidious in his bearing, yet the effect of his arrival in these places was dizzying. Hearts fluttered, senses went haywire, Lady

Rosebery almost fainted and Lady Mildmay said that when he spoke to [her] in a doorway [her] heart beat so violently that [she] could hardly answer him. What can he have said? His 'underlook', as it was called, excited them, as indeed did the rumours that he was an infidel and dreadfully perverted. His lameness, while evoking pity, also quickened desire. The combination of genius and Satanism was irresistible, all thirsting for an introduction if only to receive a lash of his bitter tongue or maybe, maybe, to feature 'in his lays'. The Duchess of Devonshire, writing to her son Augustus Foster in Washington, described the enthusiasm and curiosity that surrounded him dwarfing any mention of the war in Spain or Portugal, flattered and praised wherever he appeared. One lady, Annabella Milbanke, sighting him in that intoxicating season of his fame, found him 'wanting in the calm benevolence that would touch [her] heart', though she would go on to fall in love with him.

In the daytime, to offset the hazards of nightly revels, he boxed with Gentleman Jackson, fenced with Henry Angelo and had Fletcher rub him down with liniments in order that he could reappear that same evening with the air of 'cool languor' that he cultivated.

In his dark clothes, exuding an air of mystery, his whole appearance was a testimony to the cureless wound within. Even women barred by class and by circumstance from these gilded salons sought to introduce themselves to Byron and he was inundated with declarations of love. Oh yes, their motives, they each insisted, were totally honourable, they wished only to reach the poetic soul of Childe Harold, whom Byron himself deemed 'a repulsive personage'.

'You whom everybody loves or wishes to love' the courtesan Harriette Wilson wrote, asking if they might meet alone, her letters bearing the seal of a cupid. She knew he was clever, she knew he was unhappy, but whatever his faults or defects, her honest heart was prepared to love him. He was Poet, Devil and God, attributes that appealed to every woman, but especially her, pleading that she might once hope to kiss him before he died. Henrietta d'Ussieres, receiving no reply to her effusions on gilt-edged notepaper tied with blue ribbon, said that if he wished her not to continue writing to him, he had only to send his servant to the 'penny post office in Mount Street' to tell the clerk that he wished no more correspondence from her, but that if he kept silent, then she would go on writing to him. She too believed she was his Thyrza. Touching on a future scenario, she cast herself as 'the sister whom he love[d]' but did not realise it. True to his unpredictability, Byron did put pen to paper and reading it, Henrietta yielded to 'breathless palpitations', she was ready to bare her soul. She was a mountain girl with a touch of the savage in her, had had a fraught upbringing, had been married at a young age to a superannuated rake and claimed to have met Napoleon in Lausanne, who spoke 'soothing words' to her after she was almost trampled on by the horse of his aide-de-camp. She imagined herself in his rooms, moving about on tiptoe, arranging his papers while he wrote his 'angelic verses'. However, when they did meet, her fluster was great, having encountered Byron the man, rather than Byron the poet, and all illusion was shattered.

TEN

From 1812 to 1814, at the peak of his fame, Byron's heart, as he said, was always alighting on the nearest perch and there were many perches at his disposal.

The fugue of women involved with him included Lady Melbourne, his *tactique* confidante and co-conspirator; Lady Caroline Lamb, her daughter-in-law; Lady Oxford, his half-sister Augusta Leigh, Lady Frances Webster and Annabella Milbanke. To Lady Melbourne he wrote three and four times a day, enclosing copies of all the love letters he was receiving, flattering her, adding that if she were younger she would turn his head as she had indeed turned his heart; and to Annabella Milbanke, her niece and his future wife, he would in one of his treacherous boasts, claim of having had 'criminal connections with the old Lady', at her instigation, though she being old, he hardly knew how to set about it. But in 1812 at the zenith of his fame, he was her 'creature'. Lady Melbourne was not a woman of great virtue, but she knew how to conduct an affair in those gladiatorial circles. She had been married at sixteen to Sir Peniston Lamb, who presently took a mistress, inculcating in her a withering cynicism. With her friend Georgiana, Duchess of Devonshire, she had sat for Daniel Gardner's portrait *Macbeth, Witches round the Cauldron.* She did not languish in marital doldrums, became a 'favourite' of the Prince of Wales and mistress of Lord Egremont, to whom she bore two children. Her son William Lamb, whom she was grooming for a political career, was having an affair with Caroline's mother, Lady Bessborough, when he sighted her, at the age of thirteen, deciding that she was by far the most ravishing and covetable of the Devonshire set.

Byron's affair with 'Caro, the little volcano', lasted under five months, incurring a disproportionate amount of attention at the time and subsequently the subject of biographies, novels including *Glenarvon*, penned by the aggrieved lady herself, in which Byron the anti-hero is accredited with every crime from murder to incest to infanticide, but as he said he had not sat long enough for the portrait.

Lady Caroline and he seemed destined for each other, both aristocratic, preening and disdainful. Wildly unconventional, Caro often dressed in the scarlet and sepia livery of her pages and in her commonplace book, gave herself the nicknames of Sprite, Ariel, Titania and Little Fairy Queen. As with every other young woman, she was agog to meet the author of *Childe Harold*, since author and fictional hero were interchangeable. Samuel Rogers, a banker and poet whose poems were, according to Byron, 'all sugar and sago', had given her a copy of *Childe Harold*, which so enthralled her that she resolved she must meet him, even if he was as ugly as Aesop.

She dispatched an anonymous letter to Byron, suggested they meet at Hookham's Bookshop and maybe indulge in a 'drop', while also implying that she was married and a woman of consequence. On first seeing him at Lady Westmorland's, surrounded by so many beautiful and designing women, Caro turned on her heel and declined to be presented, leaving him somewhat piqued. A few days later, returning from a gallop in Hyde Park, all 'filthy' and 'heated', as she sat with Tom Moore and Rogers, Byron was announced. She flew out of the room to change her habit and returned in a beautiful diaphanous gown, the sort of dress she wore at the waltzing parties in Melbourne House and Almack's Club, where heiresses went in search of husbands and married women in search of dalliances to avenge their ever-faithless husbands. The imperial waltz, imported from the Rhine, was all the rage, Byron however detesting it, since he could not himself dance, and in a scathing verse rebuked the wanton willing limbs and the grotesque figure of the Prince of Wales, who 'with his princely paunch' was regarded as an expert waltzer.

However, he was captivated by Caro, her boyish good looks, her pale gold bobbed hair, her bewitching voice and intermittent lisp. She claimed not to know where bread and butter came from, ate only off silver and believed that England was comprised of marquises, earls and beggars. She and her husband William Lamb lived under the same roof as the scrutinous Lady Melbourne, a strategy which both mother-in-law and husband resolved upon, to curb some of Caro's wilder sallies. At her wedding to William she had a hysterical fit, tore her wedding gown and collapsed at the altar. She would later, in a scalding letter, tell her mother-in-law that William was a flagellist, that he had schooled her in the most unusual sexual deviations and sabotaged the few virtues that she had possessed.

Before the evening ended Byron asked if he could meet her alone and next day she ordered that a rope handrail be fitted to the three flights of stone stairs to serve as an impromptu banister. The first roses and carnations which he sent her carried a note alluding to the fact that 'Her Ladyship' liked everything that was new and rare. These flowers, dried and preserved, were found in a book in her room in Melbourne House after her death in 1828. Byron's visits were tolerated by husband and mother-in-law because they believed, as with all her cravings, her passions would subside. She already had had an affair with Sir Godfrey Webster, who gave her a farewell gift of a dog, which bit her six-year-old son Augustus. Byron would arrive at eleven in the morning and sit with her in the tiny bedroom that overlooked St James's Park, where she was to be found opening her letters, choosing her dresses for the day or playing ball with little Augustus, whose sickness was believed to be a consequence of hereditary syphilis. She had cancelled her waltzing mornings.

To his male friends Byron was penning jaunty bulletins of the progress he was making, but his letters to her allow for no doubt of his having fallen in love –

> Then your heart, my poor Caro (what a little volcano!), that pours *lava* through your veins; and yet I cannot wish it a bit colder ... you know I have always thought you the cleverest, most agreeable, absurd, amiable, perplexing, dangerous, fascinating little being that lives now, or ought to have lived 2000 years ago. I won't talk to you of beauty; I am no judge. But our beauties cease to be so when near you, and therefore you have either some, or something better.

Her heart and all else did not only meet his, but flew before it and never would she forget when he first kissed her in the carriage and drew her to him 'like a magnet'. At its zenith, he decided they should elope, a proposal she thrilled to, proving herself to be surprisingly practical, even arranging to sell her jewels to go to the ends of the earth with him, but Byron was already hesitating. She had grown supine, the very haughtiness, the disdain, the unpredictability that had intrigued him were no more. A clinging Caro, she was 'the unworthy sunflower basking in the light of the unclouded Sun God'. He had misread his little *enfant terrible.* In a chastened letter he wrote to say 'the dream and delirium must pass away, the veil of illusion must be lifted from [their] eyes, a month's absence and [they] would become rational'.

She would have none of it. She did foolish, precipitous and humiliating things. No longer Ariel or Titania, she was 'poor Caro William' whom hostesses were ridiculing in their smug exchanges between one another. She laid siege to Byron. She made friends with Fletcher so as to gain admittance to Byron's rooms in St James's Street, to rifle through his letters and journals for evidence of betrayal, she would plead to be asked to suppers where he had been asked and if refused she would wait in the garden or talk to the coachmen, believing that her status set her above ridicule, except that it didn't. Dallas describes a page in scarlet Hussar jacket and pantaloons, appearing in Byron's rooms, the light hair curling about the face and a fancy hat in the hand, who turned out not to be a page but Caroline herself in disguise. Byron sat mutely, because he disliked scenes, but he was also fascinated by Caro's androgyny and powerless to tear himself completely away from her mischiefs and her declared transgressions with her pages, male and female. Hobhouse describes another incursion, thunderous raps on the door, Caroline climbing the garret stairs in a man's heavy overcoat with a page's attire underneath, shouting that there would be blood spilt, if Byron tried to escape from her. She still believed she could win him back and Hobhouse, knowing Byron's vacillating temperament, also feared such an outcome.

Byron himself shilly-shallied, saying at one point that there was no alternative but for him and Caroline to go away together. Hobhouse, with the help of the shopkeeper downstairs, escorted her out of there into a series of carriages and eventually she was brought back to her distraught mother and her incensed mother-in-law. Next day, Byron received a cutting of her auburn pubic hair tinged with blood, asking that he send the same in return, his wild antelope adding, 'I asked you not to send blood but yet do – because if it means love I like to have it.' Her capriciousness knew no bounds, she would be missing, she would be found hiding in a chemist's in Pall Mall or selling her opal ring to take a stagecoach to Portsmouth, refusing Lady Bessborough's plea that they go to Ireland, then claiming that she was pregnant and that with a long journey there she might miscarry. The Prince of Wales, hearing of these lunacies, as indeed everyone had, claimed that Byron had bewitched the whole Melbourne household, mothers, mothers-in-law and daughters all, making fools of them. Lady Bessborough finally made her decision and so mother, daughter and Sir William set out for one of the Bessborough estates in County Waterford in Ireland.

Byron shed tears of agitation at their parting and his farewell letter to her, which she kept to the end of her days, confirms him as one of the most ardent lovers on the page – 'Do you think now I am cold and stern and artful? ... "Promise not to love you!" Ah, Caroline, it is past promising ... You know

I would with pleasure give up all here and all beyond the grave for you ...'

Caroline was devastated, a cousin who met them en route described her as 'worn to the bone, pale as death, her eyes staring out of her head', while William laughed away and ate like a trooper.

With the rolling seas between them, Byron could afford to be gallant, though Lady Melbourne is advocating ruthlessness, better as she put it a little present pain to avoid future ruin. To Caro he dispatched 'absurdities' to keep her gay, his equilibrium somewhat rattled when she reminded him that only eight guineas and the mail boat lay between them or when her letters became more threatening. She also began a correspondence with her detested mother-in-law Lady Melbourne, wishing it known and therefore relayed to Byron that she had kept his letters, brimming as they did with passion. Byron quaked at the thought that a volley of intemperate and by now hollow declarations would be exposed to the world. Marriage, he decided, was the only way to escape from her, and marriage within three weeks at that. Fletcher, his valet since his youth, who had travelled with him to the Levant, proposed a Dutch widow who had moved to London, 'a woman of great riches and rotundity', her little maid Abigail a possible catch for Fletcher himself.

Byron had set his sights elsewhere.

At one of the waltz parties in Melbourne House, Caroline in full plumage, Byron had noticed another young woman, unattached, a little plump and decidedly reserved. This was Annabella Milbanke, Lady Melbourne's philosophically minded niece. In her diary that same evening, Annabella did not dilate on his being her fate, instead she described a mouth that betrayed an acrimonious spirit, a man full of disdain which he did not always try to conceal. In a letter to her mother she said that she had made no overtures at the shrine of *Childe Harold*, while conceding that she would not refuse the offer of his acquaintance. Byron noted her apparent modesty, her fresh complexion, her round pink cheeks which were in contrast to the artificiality of most of the ladies present; however, he mistook her for a lady's companion rather than an heiress in her own right. It was Tom Moore who apprised him of her fortune and said, 'Marry her and repair Newstead.'

'I was, am and shall be I fear attached to another, one to whom I have never said much', so he announced to Lady Melbourne. Surprised at it being her gauche niece, her crisp retort was that poor Annabella's looks might improve if she should be in love with him. Nevertheless and despite her possessiveness of him, she thought marriage might free him from Caroline, whose spell he had not fully thrown off, and also she was flattered at his declared delight at the pleasure of being able to call her 'aunt'. It was she, on Byron's behalf, who dispatched the formal proposal and it was to her the disappointing reply came – 'Believing that he will never be the object of that strong affection which could make me happy in domestic life I should wrong him by any measure that might even indirectly confirm his present impressions.' Byron could, Annabella added, excite affection perhaps in her, but she was uncertain if he could inspire esteem. However, to her friend Lady Gosford, she confessed to being in a state of high excitement and felt the necessity to alter the channel of her feelings.

Byron took the refusal blithely, said she would have been a cold collation, whereas he preferred hot suppers. Lady

Melbourne, at her own initiative, decided to pursue matters, asking Annabella what qualities she would require in a husband. Annabella followed with a list that included duty, strong and generous feelings, reason, economy, manners rather than beauty, adding that she would not 'enter into a family where there is a strong tendency to Insanity'. Lady Melbourne replied, saying it was doubtful that Annabella would ever find a person worthy to be her husband while she remained on her stilts, reminding her that marriage was a sort of lottery.

Byron, buoyed somewhat by the supposed sale of Newstead, believed that he was about to receive £25,000 from the deposit paid by Mr Claughton, a Lancashire lawyer; he decided to go to Cheltenham to take the spa waters, resume his rigorous fasting for his various maladies and avail himself of the society ladies, all of whom went there in September, sated from the summer revels. Mr Claughton however only paid £5,000, a sum which Byron after a lapse of years, felt obligated to repay to Scrope Davies, but he set out for Cheltenham anyhow. His first female consolation was an Italian songstress with dark eyes and a poetical voice, who spoke no English, which for Byron was a blessing. Their dalliance was marred only by her huge appetite, consuming chicken wings, sweetbreads, custards, peaches and port wine, an affront to the 24-year-old poet who had told Lady Melbourne that ladies should only partake of lobster salad and champagne.

But Caro had not fallen silent or been locked away, as Byron might have hoped. Express letters flowed from her, castigation, abject pleadings or boasts of the men who did love her, the Duke's mob and all the Waterford swains. Byron was advising her to curb her vanity, which was ridiculous, and to exert her caprices on some new conquest, he himself having gained the attentions of a most egalitarian lady.

ELEVEN

Lady Oxford, formerly Lady Jane Elizabeth Scott, a rector's daughter, beautiful, enlightened and unconventional, had, as she would tell Byron, been forced into marriage at the age of twenty-two, to the fifth Earl of Oxford, an out-and-out dullard. She had given her favours to other men quite soon after marriage and her children were sired by five different men. Her husband, with an estimable complacency, was said to have forgiven her, being so struck by her candour and frank confession. Lady Oxford considered herself an intellectual, was a stalwart of the Whig Party and a member of the Hampden Club, where gentlemen radicals and blackguards mingled in the wan hope of reforming one another. She professed to live her life according to the tenets of Jean-Jacques Rousseau and so she would become Byron's enchantress and 'titular genius'. She urged him to be more politicised, something to which he was not tractable, seldom seen in the House of Lords, where he made only three speeches, one on behalf of the Nottingham weavers and the second on behalf of five million Irish Catholics whose condition he said was worse than that of black slaves. He had gone there reluctantly from a dinner party and by his wit and invective, kept the House in roars of laughter through the night, his presence however providing that majority of one for the motion to be passed.

Lady Oxford was thirty-eight when she and Byron met, her ripe charms suggesting to him a Claude Lorrain painting at sunset, its last dying beams having a singular radiance. He was invited to spend two months at their country mansion, Eywood, in Herefordshire, and soon unwisely relays to Lady Melbourne that he is in the 'bowers of Armida'. Sensing her chagrin he wrote again to reassure her that *her* spells for him retained their full force. The countryside is wild and beautiful, Byron plays blind man's buff with Lady Oxford's children, they go sightseeing, days and nights are passed in unparalleled quiet and contentment and he has not yawned once, which is a phenomenon for him. How gratifying it would be for us to have a picture of those drawing rooms, those galleries and staircases where servants came and went, privy to so many indiscretions, to know what Lady Oxford, the 'enchantress', wore for dinner or how draughty it might have been in the big dining room when Lord Oxford's elderly aunts, who lived upstairs in retirement, were allowed down. But Byron does not tell us, having no time for domestic minutiae, since his tastes were for the more grandiose.

There were days when he felt that perhaps he should be setting out for London, but then the roads were flooded and anyhow his male friends in the capital were preoccupied with politics and debt and gout. He had cast himself as Rinaldo in Tasso's *Gerusalemme*, whose amours kept him from his duties as a crusader.

He had been pleading with Lady Melbourne, his 'dear Machiavel', to manage Caro and since it proved fruitless, he decided on harsher measures, resolving to become 'as treacherous as Talleyrand'. Caroline had asked for a lock of his hair and instead he had sent one of Lady Oxford's, along with her seal, which bore her initials. Recognising it, Caroline was aghast. Lady Oxford had been her dear friend. Had they not conducted a literary correspondence, cogitating on whether Greek purified or inflamed the passions, and now that selfsame friend, her mentor, her Aspasia, had deceived her. She dashes off a letter, a 'German tirade' as he called it, to Lady Oxford, to force the truth, to know what is between them. Lady Oxford does not condescend to reply, but when the threats become more urgent, when couriers arrive with twenty-page letters, when Caro threatens to inform Lord Oxford himself and worse to call on them, Byron is told by his balmy mistress to sever the connection. He does so in a manner that could only succeed in unhinging Caro even more – 'Our affections are not in our power,' he wrote. 'My opinion of you is entirely altered . . . I love another.'

Within a week the postmark is from Holyhead, signalling that Caro and family are returning. En route, she has collapsed and has had to be bled and leeched at 'the filthy Dolphin Inn' in Cornwall. Once installed at Brocket Hall, the Melbourne country estate, she insists that they should meet but is refused. She is asking for a ring and trinkets that she gave him to be returned. Byron no longer has them as, unwisely, he has given them to Lady Charlotte, Lady Oxford's eleven-year-old daughter, for whom he had formed an unhealthy passion, something her mother summarily put a stop to.

Caro was insatiate. She gave herself the name of Phryne, Horace's vengeful Roman courtesan. She was seen riding wildly on the turnpikes of Hertfordshire, near Brocket Hall, had *Ne Crede B* – in contradiction of his family motto *Crede Byron* – inscribed on the buttons of her servants' livery and wheedled a miniature of Byron, which was meant for Lady Oxford, from his publisher John Murray. She staged an auto-da-fé in the gardens at Brocket Hall, whereby an effigy of Byron met the same fate as that of Guy Fawkes. Young girls from the nearby village of Welwyn were recruited, dressed in white and put to dance around a fire onto which an exulting Caro, half Ophelia, half Lady Macbeth, threw copies of Byron's letters, along with rings, flowers and trinkets, while her pages recited the verse she had composed –

> Burn, fire, burn,
> While wondering boys exclaim,
> And gold and trinkets glitter in the flame.

The brutal letter in which he had said 'Our affections are not in our power – mine are engaged. I love another' would be embodied in her sensational novel, *Glenarvon*, written in a feverish month and published in 1816, much to the chagrin of London society, whom she also pilloried. Hobhouse noted that the novel 'rendered the vicious little author more odious if possible than ever'. The Melbournes had her declared insane and persuaded William to divorce her, except that on the morning he was to sign the necessary papers, Caroline was seen sitting on his lap feeding him bread and butter. When Byron read it in Geneva, after his exile, he merely said, 'I read *Glenarvon* too . . . God Damn.'

While Caroline's vengeance was in full spate, in 1812 and 1813, Lady Melbourne was still urging her son William to seek a divorce, except that he hesitated. He cannot have been too displeased at seeing Byron, a man he hated, mauled and humiliated by his wife. Years later, when he became Prime Minister, he told Queen Victoria that Byron 'was treacherous beyond conception ... he dazzled everybody and deceived them'.

Byron and Lady Oxford would both say that for those seven or eight months they lived like 'the gods of Lucretius', their harmony shattered only by a slight distress when Lady Oxford thought she was pregnant, jolting Lord Oxford from his pusillanimous and admirable tolerance. It turned out to be a false alarm, but a certain dimming of the passions ensued and in that mysterious way in which marriages can be redeemed, Lord and Lady Oxford, by then heavily in debt, sailed for the Continent, leaving a somewhat peeved Lord Byron behind, who confessed to Lady Melbourne that he was more 'Carolinish' than he could have imagined.

A new sensation he might call it, an emotional hurricane would be more precise. Augusta Leigh, Byron's half-sister and five years his senior, has been variously depicted as scatterbrained, a moral idiot and a schemer, her childhood as fractured and peripatetic as Byron's own. Her mother Amelia fell in love with the charismatic Mad Jack, Byron's father, and when she told her husband, Lord Carmarthen, that she was leaving him and their three children, he is said 'to have fainted away three times'. Soon after Augusta was born, Amelia, still infatuated with the errant Mad Jack, rose too soon from her confinement to follow him on a hunt. She caught a lingering disease and died on Augusta's first birthday and her child was raised by her aristocratic relatives. Byron and Augusta had met only occasionally down the years and at Cambridge he had enlisted her in his vendettas against the woman he was 'ashamed to call mother'. However, he felt an affinity for her and believed that between them there existed a mystical thread.

Now, at the zenith of his fame, Augusta is asking for his

help. Her husband, Colonel George Leigh, former equerry of the Prince of Wales, a man of the turf, an habitué of the gaming tables, charming to women and overbearing to subordinates, is mired in debt. Arriving in London in April 1813, she had to leave her house at Six Mile Bottom near Newmarket in Cambridgeshire to escape the bailiffs, her three children elsewhere and her husband on an extended visit to his racing friends.

Byron, though still smarting from Lady Oxford's defection, is pleased at the announcement of her arrival and has asked Lady Melbourne to get him a 'she-voucher' for Almack's Dancing Palace in King Street, a hundred-foot assembly room to which only the privileged were admitted. Augusta is in his rooms in Bennett Street, his books and his sabres along the walls, rooms where women were rarely admitted, tired from the coach journey, somewhat dowdy, given to blushing and shy as a hare, like Byron himself. She is to stay with her cousin, the Hon. Theresa Villiers, in nearby Berkeley Street and already Byron is promising to watch over her as if she were an unmarried woman. Her presence is soon a delight, that softening influence that he always sought in women, Augusta making the short journey each day to be with him, chatty, pliant and silly with her large grey eyes and her baby talk, she seems to understand him as no woman previously had. It's crinkum and crankum and laughter, pulling him out of his grumps, and the lame foot that he had so determinedly hidden from all others, not hidden from her and christened by them 'the little foot'. And so it is Guss and Goose and Baby Byron and foolery and giggles, Augusta wearing the new dresses and silk shawls he has bought for her, the thrill of showing her off to the acerbic hostesses, home in his carriage at five or six in the morning, gabbling, mimicking the hoi polloi and somehow it happened, the transition from affection to something untoward. Never, he said, 'was seduction so easy'. They are besotted, they are in love, they are confused, travelling from London to Six Mile Bottom, then back to London again, making irrational plans to go abroad. Soon there are hints to his friends, Lady Melbourne informed of the Gordian knot tied too close to his heart, and to Tom Moore he writes, 'I am, at this moment, in a far more serious and entirely new scrape than any of the last twelvemonths, and that is saying a great deal.'

To himself he admits that this love is a mixture of good and diabolical as all passions are. He gives Colonel Leigh £1,000, cancels a passage that he was to make alone on a ship and prepares to elope with Augusta, possibly to Sicily. Augusta wishes to bring one of her daughters with her, but Byron detests children and says anyhow a child can be conceived on the spot. Confiding in her few friends, Augusta is told to recall her mother's madness at leaving a husband for Mad Jack and precipitating her own death. Lady Melbourne, her suspicions founded, tells him, 'If you do not retreat, you are lost forever, it is a crime for which there is no forgiveness in this world or in the next.' The plans to travel begin to falter. There is a plague across Europe, there is their mounting trepidation and the condemnation of the world waiting to fall upon them. He resolves to go away anyhow, to cut himself off from her, a passage in any ship, Cadiz, St Petersburg, Italy, anywhere. Deeply in debt, horrified at casting up his moral accounts, he nevertheless prepares for this flight by ordering swords, guns, mahogany dressing boxes, writing desks, uniforms, umpteen pairs of nankeen trousers, scarlet officers' coats, gold epaulettes, snuff boxes, telescopes and precious gifts for Mussulman nobles.

Lady Melbourne warns him never to return to Six Mile Bottom, he does anyhow, leaves after twenty-four hours, he and Scrope Davies that night consuming six bottles of claret and burgundy in Cambridge. He returned to London a distraught man. Bizarrely, he resumes a correspondence with Annabella Milbanke, saying that on the score of friendship he cannot trust himself as he could not help but love her. His doctor, unsurprisingly, diagnoses an awryness of mind and body, emotions out of compass, which he ascribes to a life of prodigal excesses. To vanquish his 'demon', which is to say the conquering of his love for Augusta, he accepts an invitation from his Cambridge friend, 'that fool of fools', Sir Wedderburn Webster.

TWELVE

Sir Wedderburn, that 'glorious object for cuckoldom', recently married to Lady Frances, daughter of the Earl of Mountnorris, invited Byron to visit them at Aston Hall, near Rotherham in Yorkshire. Augusta, at Byron's request, has also been invited, but she declines, now finding herself pregnant and therefore queasy and also guessing that she might be a wallflower in that company. Accepting, Byron requests that he be excused from going to the races at Doncaster and also from dining with them, as he does not dine at all.

The ensuing farcical goings-on, what with misplaced passion and clandestine glances, could easily have been penned by the playwright Richard Brinsley Sheridan, whom Byron greatly admired.

Lady Frances proves to be pretty and pleasing, but in delicate health and according to Byron, 'close to decline'. Webster, 'jealous to jaundice', gives orations on his wife's beauty, kisses her hand several times at table, overtures which she receives with a noticeable lifelessness. The other guests are frightful, facetious and frivolous. Byron, despite his earlier demur, does attend dinners, Webster droning on about his wife's virtues and high principles, comparing her morals to Christ, at which Byron, fortified with claret, laughs so exceedingly that his host is outraged and harmony only restored because as Byron said the devil himself thought it proper to do so. Daily missives are dispatched to Lady Melbourne and for secrecy's sake the denomination of 'Ph' is given to Lady Frances, whose virtue must be preserved.

Webster warns Byron that 'femme' must not see Byron's copies of Dante or Alfieri, which would do her infinite damage. Yet 'femme' is beginning to show a certain interest in Byron, evidenced by her eyes, her change of colour, a trembling hand and a devotional attitude. Meanwhile, Webster, the Othello monopolist, who in his leisure time writes pamphlets, expounds at table on what he would do to any man who gazed too long at his wife or sought to compromise her – he would exterminate such a brute. Byron concludes to Lady Melbourne that his throat might soon be cut, but vows to retaliate with a 'roughing' and with shaming Webster by citing the country wenches that he has been pursuing.

Augusta's frantic letters go unanswered, as Byron has found another perch.

The topography of the house however is not ideal for the putative but by now more manifest lovers. In the billiards room, 'amidst the clashing of billiard balls and the barking Nettle', a poodle which the Websters have given Byron as a present, a declaration is made. Ph asks Byron how a woman who liked a man could inform him of it. Imprudently, as he tells Lady Melbourne and 'in tender and tolerably turned prose', he risks all by writing a letter. He hands it to Ph in the billiards room, when, to their consternation, 'Marito', whom Byron wished at the bottom of the Red Sea, enters, but the Lady with great presence of mind deposits the letter inside her gown and close to her heart. So begins another amatory correspondence under Webster's roof, Byron also writing to Annabella Milbanke, addressing her as 'My dear friend'. For Byron, Ph's letters, which he leaves on the desk in his bedroom, reek too much of virtue and the soul, but then again she is a woman who takes prayers morning and night and as he tells Lady Melbourne, 'is measured for a Bible every quarter'. Yet he can report that they have, in a sense, 'made love' and that Platonism is in peril. All that is needed is the privacy to consummate it. Apart from Sir Wedderburn's vigilance, which is manic, Byron also suspects one of the other male guests of having cast himself in the Iago mode, and her sister Lady Catherine, recently jilted, seems to cling over-duly to Ph.

It is decided that the house party will repair to Newstead, the 'melancholy mansion' of Byron's forebears and where he hopes the residing genii will foster his intentions. During dinner Ph announces to her husband that her sister shall share her room at Newstead, whereupon Webster thunders about his rights and maintains that none but a husband has any legal claim to divide the spouse's pillow. Lady Frances, in a rare moment of spiritedness, whispers to Byron – 'N'importe, this is all nothing', a remark which perplexes him greatly. At Newstead he has one of the mounted skulls filled with claret, which he downs in one go, incurring a fit which bars him from being with the ladies, convulsions followed by such motionlessness that Fletcher believes that his master is dead. But his master revives in order to resume the courtship.

The opportunity at last presents itself. It is two in the morning at Newstead and they are alone, Ph's words so sincere, so serious, she is in a perplexity of love, she owns up to a helplessness, saying she will give herself to him but fears that she will 'not survive the fall'. Byron is flabbergasted, he is used to women saying no while meaning yes, and this sincerity, this artlessness, this ingenuousness is too much altogether so that he wavers and in a burst of chivalry that he would come to regret, he feels he cannot take advantage of her. Each and every nuance is relayed to the scrutinous Lady Melbourne, who of course is impatient to know if he is willing to go away with Ph. The answer is Yes. To the ends of the earth if necessary, because he loves her, adding that if he had not loved her he would have been more selfish when she yielded.

When the party return to Aston Hall, the entire household is thrown into bile and ill temper, Sir Wedderburn prating at servants in front of the guests, sermonising his wife and her sister in front of the guests, and a general feeling that something catastrophic is about to occur.

What transpires is that Byron is due to leave, Frances's heart, though broken, is cemented to his as she gives him the gift of a seal, asks that he be faithful to her and vow that they meet in the spring.

On the eve of departure, Sir Wedderburn plays a caddish card, tells his wife that Byron confessed to him that he had only come and stayed to seek the hand of Lady Catherine, the drooping sister. Ph is devastated. Byron has deceived her. There is weeping and gnashing at their last secret rendezvous in the garden. Then Webster borrows £1,000 from his befuddled houseguest. The following morning as Byron prepares to step into his carriage, Webster confounds matters by professing such a friendship that he will accompany Byron to London. On the wearisome journey, Webster assures him that he and his wife are totally in love and marriage the happiest of all possible estates.

Meanwhile, Lady Frances has begun her copious correspondence, penning letters that extend to eighteen pages, dilating on Byron's beauty and her 'bursting heart'. Borne out in a poem, 'Concealed Griefs', Lady Melbourne, who is privy to this dotage, does not doubt Ph's sincerity, but pronounces her 'childish and tiresome'.

Byron had not, as he believed, exorcised the love of Augusta and with his mind in such 'a state of fermentation' he was obliged to discharge it in rhyme. A first draft of *The Bride of Abydos* was completed in four days, the 'lines strung as fast as minutes'. It recounts the passion and doomed love of Princess Zuleika and her brother Selim, Zuleika lamenting her solitary plight as she is banished to a tower. Fear of detection, as he wrote to Dr E.D. Clarke at that time, and his recent intrigue in the north, induced him to alter the consanguinity of the lovers and confine them to cousinship.

'Dear sacred name, rest ever unrevealed' Byron wrote, borrowing from, though misquoting, Pope's poem *Eloisa to Abelard*. Though the names and the narrative were ascribed to the East, the emotional turmoil certainly belonged in Bennett Street, with traces of Augusta everywhere and his inability to break with her. Publish it he must, suggesting to John Murray that it might steal quietly into the world with *The Giaour*, which featured a Venetian noble, intent on the rescue of a slave girl, Leila, from the harem of her vicious pasha. Deferring to the mores of the time, while realising that it would weaken its inner voltage, Byron agreed to make a change in *The Bride*, so as to remove the frightful taboo of incest. Brother and sister were altered to being first cousins. Though not a poet, Augusta felt compelled to respond to it in verse and by not being a poet her reply is all the more moving. Writing in French and with a haunting poignancy, she wished to share all his feelings, to see through his eyes, to live only for him, he being the only destiny that could make her happy. In the sheet of paper she had also enclosed a curl of her chestnut hair, tied with white silk. Byron kept it all his life and on the folded paper wrote 'La Chevelure of the one I most *loved*'. Her signature ended with the branches of a cross, the mathematical symbol confirming the secret of their love, and Byron had two seals made for a brooch that they would wear.

Within three months the love for Lady Frances had waned and hearing that he was with his sister, she envied that 'happy happy woman' and hoped that Augusta would not despise her. In vain and on bended knees she asked for her letters to be returned, but the request was ignored. He had tired of her, her constancy and her naiveté. Her tedious use of *aimer* merely confirmed for him the blindness of nature.

THIRTEEN

In January 1814 the River Trent was frozen, the Great North Road heaped with snowdrifts as Byron's carriage wended its perilous way north, to Newstead Abbey. Augusta, 'big with bairn', was with him and it would be her first visit to their ancestral home. The four weeks they would spend there constituted a honeymoon for them both, Byron saying, 'We never yawn or disagree, and laugh more than is suitable to so solid a mansion.' The snow swirled outside, the footpaths and oak trees were thick with it, the oak trees weighed down and Joe Murray kept fires crackling in rooms, corridors and bedrooms. The coal, as Byron reported, was excellent, the wine cellar was full and his head emptied of all his London cares.

In his bulletins to Lady Melbourne, which were half swagger and half confession, he admitted that the kind of feeling which had lately absorbed him had 'a mixture of the terrible which renders all passion insipid to a degree'. He was speaking, or rather intimating, his love for his sister, 'the one soft breast he knew'. It was one part innocence because of their missed companionship in childhood, but it was also damnation. Any error Augusta might have committed was his fault entirely, Augusta was not aware of her peril until it was too late.

Those weeks in which Augusta was wife and sister to him were the happiest of his life. She sympathised with his black moods and the violent arc of his feelings, saw the loaded pistols kept beside his bed and witnessed the nightmares in which he cried out, sometimes beset by a ghost. She ministered to him, loved him and put a napkin between his teeth because he ground them so in his sleep. In short, she was not afraid of him.

The Corsair, which Mr Murray had just published, was an immediate success and Byron once again seen as a celebrity. It was a Turkish tale 'scribbled' during his disquietude while he believed himself to be in love with both Lady Frances and Augusta. Byron used a motto from Tasso to describe Conrad the Pirate – 'Within him his thoughts cannot sleep.' A man of mystery and loneliness, he is espoused to Medora, the fair Penelope waiting in her tower, and Gulnare, the dark bewitching Circe, imprisoned in a harem by Pacha Seyd. Conrad manages to rescue Gulnare, whereupon she falls madly in love with him and murders her Pacha. He cannot escape the fact that lovers become murderers, something true for both men and women, he causing Medora to die of a broken heart, and Gulnare in her love-frenzy, the murderer of Seyd. The scenario of two women fighting for the love of a man would be re-enacted in Byron's life, between Augusta and Annabella Milbanke, Byron himself pitched into a similar hideous 'sepulchre' as Conrad was, doomed to a wandering life.

The predictable indignation from the Tory press was 'vehement and unceasing loud', Conrad, the alter ego of Byron, called an infidel and a devil was likened to Richard III, wringing from him the crisp rejoinder that 'lame animals cover best'. But these cavils and calumnies were mitigated by a rapturous letter from John Murray: 'I believe I have now sold 13,000 Copies, a thing perfectly unprecedented & the more grateful to me too as every buyer returns with looks of satisfaction & expressions of delight.' Princess Charlotte, he added, had devoured it twice in the course of the day, but its fame spread beyond royal circles and there was not a man in the street 'who [had] not read or heard-read *The Corsair*'. Some passages, as Murray noted, were 'written in gold', a gold that Robert Dallas was still the lucky recipient of.

The idyll in the snows could not last. The pain of their parting was unbearable for them both. For him she was a being 'wined around his heart in every possible manner, dearest and deepest in hope and in memory'. For her she said that if she could live and die there and be buried with him within Newstead's ruins, they would both have been happy. But Colonel Leigh, her 'lord and president', required her home and moreover, she had to prepare for the birth of the child that was due in April.

Back in his cheerless rooms in Bennett Street, many things conspired to add to his despondency. Rumours of his affair with Augusta were rife and boys at Eton asked her nephew if Augusta was the heroine Zuleika in *The Bride of Abydos*. Hobhouse and Douglas Kinnaird exchanged 'frightful suspicions of it' and at gatherings in Holland House Byron himself spoke rashly of a woman he was in love with and who was with child, saying that the child would be called Medora.

But above and beyond all the given reproaches, there was his tormented state of mind or, as he put it in a letter to

Lady Melbourne – 'All these externals are nothing to that within.'

The correspondence with Annabella Milbanke had been staggering on, Byron telling himself that he wanted a companion and a friend because he had had enough of love. Despite her moral rectitude, she wrote to say how much she admired *The Giaour*, which Byron had called 'a snake of a poem', because of the way it extended its rattles. Her admiration for it may have stemmed from the fact that the hero, whom she associated with Byron himself, was haunted by ill deeds – 'So writhes the mind remorse hath riven.' In *The Giaour* the hero is haunted by the image of the drowned girl Leila, and the severed arm of Hassan, whom he had had to kill, just as Byron himself was haunted by the crime of incest, which though Shelley may have described 'as a very poetical circumstance', Byron was teetering. Resolving now to vanquish his 'demon' and break with Augusta, he planned a trip to Holland, the 'bluff burghers' having defeated the French and declared a republic.

'... Love will find its way/Through paths where wolves would fear to prey' he had written in *The Giaour*, and in bleak and misty Seaham in the county of Durham, Annabella was indeed in love with him and wretched at being so wanting in wisdom as to have pretended that she had disposed of her heart elsewhere. This deception led to her breakdown, which brought their correspondence to an abrupt halt.

'I mark this day!' Byron wrote on 11 April 1814, as the Emperor Napoleon Bonaparte unconditionally surrendered to the combined British, Prussian and Austrian forces, having been defeated the previous year at the Battle of the Nations in Leipzig, then in March 1814 at the Battle of Laon. Now he would be exiled from Paris to the island of Elba.

Byron, as Hobhouse said, had always held 'an irrational admiration' for Napoleon, identifying with him as a mythic hero and an invincible general, high above 'the straw monarchs of England'. But his God had become a pagod. 'This imperial diamond hath a flaw in it.' He raged at his downfall, saying no man, no fiend, had fallen so far, even wishing that Napoleon had committed suicide in the noble Roman tradition. In an 'Ode to Napoleon', written in despondence and anger, he vented his muddled feelings, regretting only that the poem would give pleasure to his Tory enemies. His anger was further inflamed by the various celebrations in London, the monarchs of Europe, the Czar of Russia, King of Prussia, Prince Metternich and Marshal von Blücher, all welcomed for royal jubilations by the Prince Regent.

The paring-away of a giant to gradual insignificance was a jest of the gods and a fate that might befall himself. In a letter once to Annabella Milbanke, he had said he preferred the talent of action, of war, or the Senate or even science, to all the speculations of those mere dreamers of another existence, by which he meant poets. It was as if being a poet was not heroic enough for him, succumbing as poets did 'to the gloomy vanity of drawing from self'.

On 15 April Augusta gave birth to a daughter, whom she named Elizabeth Medora, after the heroine in *The Corsair.* With a triumphalism, he wrote to Lady Melbourne that it was worthwhile and the child had not been born an ape, a reference to the superstition that pertained towards the progeny of incestuous lovers. He went on to add that Augusta's love was what he had been seeking all his life. Yet he would not single out the child for special affection, preferring the elder sister Georgina, but Medora would in time come to believe that she was his daughter, the inheritor of his raging genius, just as she would curse her mother and describe her as a hyena who deserved to lick the dust.

Vanitas vanitatum. The old emptiness the old despair. The soirées at this or that house began to pall, were a deplorable waste of time, nothing imparted, nothing acquired, just tosh. Hobhouse predicted that Byron was becoming 'a *loup garou*', his correspondence of that time giving ample indication of a man in torment and possibly a poet in doubt with regard to his own gifts. How else can we reconcile his estimate of Edmund Kean in *Richard III* showing 'life – nature – truth without exaggeration or diminution' with his demolishing of Shakespeare, whom he had formerly lauded as that 'most extraordinary of writers'. To Mr James Hogg, the 'Ettrick Shepherd', who had written to ask for a poem to be included in a volume of poems by contemporaries, Byron wrote scaldingly – 'Shakespeare's name, you may depend on it, stands absurdly too high and will go down. He had no invention as to stories, none whatever. He took all his plots from old novels, and threw their stories into a dramatic shape, at as little expense of thought as you or I could turn his plays back again into prose tales. That he threw over whatever he did write some flashes of genius, nobody can deny: but that was all.'

To Lady Melbourne he is promising that he and Augusta will grow good, he buys a parrot and a macaw for company, announces to John Murray that he will stop writing, rescinds his decision, receives Caroline Lamb in his rooms, where she speaks of a resumed tenderness, his lips pressed to hers as he revealed his horrible secret. He is restless, agitated, either living on seltzer water and biscuits or getting drunk with Scrope Davies, sparring with Gentleman Jackson 'to attenuate and keep up the ethereal part of me'. Throughout, he pined for Augusta, wishing that like St Francis, he could be given a wife made of snow to dampen his passion.

FOURTEEN

'Hanging and marriage . . . go by Destiny' George Farquhar wrote. Byron's correspondence with Annabella Milbanke, the 'fair philosopher', had been renewed, letters in which Christianity, Horace, Tacitus and all such edifying topics were discussed, though not yet the question of marriage. Their 'epistolatory courtship' is a marvel of eloquence, verisimilitude and staggering deception. He is apologising if he is intruding too much on her time, to say nothing of her patience, he is extolling her virtues, her mind, her morals, while pleading to obtain her good opinion of him. For her part, she is melting. His poetry, even *The Bride of Abydos*, has given her more pleasure than the QEDs of Euclid. His dozy firelighter Mrs Mule could have warned him of his precipitousness, but Byron had talked himself into believing that he was in love with Annabella and she for her part, though she had sought to suppress it, had fallen in love with him at first sight, as did, almost, every woman he met. Her first circumlocutory refusal, the pretence of another 'attachment', her breakdown upon hearing that he was going abroad, all indicative of her secret torment.

He is having to listen to the 'felicitations' of newly married men, though in his view they simply have had their tails cut off. He meets the various other candidates Augusta has proposed, thinking that whoever she loved he could not help but like. One, Lady Charlotte Leveson-Gower, has 'soul', blushes easily and is soon christened the antelope, but she proves skittish and is somewhat afraid of Byron. To Augusta's dismay she vanishes when a former suitor, Henry Charles Howard, reappears and asks for her hand. More in a spirit of ennui than ardour, when they are at Newstead, Byron sends Annabella a somewhat succinct letter – 'Are the objections to which you alluded insuperable, or is there any line or change of conduct which could possibly remove them?' Augusta thought it 'a pretty letter, the prettiest letter ever', which it wasn't. According to her, Byron sat on the steps in an agitation, waiting for the post that would bring Annabella's reply.

Earlier the gardener had burst into the room in a state of excitement, having just dug up Catherine Byron's wedding ring, which had been missing for years, Byron remarking that if Annabella consented, she would be married with that ring, hardly an apposite heirloom, considering Catherine's brief and unhappy marriage. Byron, according to Augusta, 'almost fainted away with agitation' upon reading the letter of acceptance. Annabella admitted to a joy that she had despaired of and pledged herself to make his happiness her first object in life. Byron felt no such joy. His reply next day cursory, dispensing with love talk, noting that their pursuits were not unalike, since neither had a great passion for the world and hence relied on their intellectual natures, and that although 'sinning', he had also been sinned against and had long stood alone in life.

Even the most idle observer might question why the carriage was not waiting, why it took Byron almost two months to set out on the north road and make the three-hundred-mile journey to Seaham to meet with Annabella and the parents, Lady Judith and Sir Ralph, those whom he hoped to call his own. Seaham was a God-forsaken hamlet with a sprinkling of cottages and Seaham Manor, the seat of the Milbankes, propped on cliffs overlooking the choppy North Sea. She was counting the days. Mama and Papa were counting the days, Mama in one of her 'fusses' and Sir Ralph choosing the wines for the august visit. Yet 'petty casualties and melancholy accidents' got in Byron's way. So many things got in the way, the least of them being poetry. There was the matter of the marriage settlement, which had to be left 'to the men of parchment', his solicitor Mr Hanson and her father's solicitor Mr Hoar having much to discuss, except that Mr Hanson and Mr Hoar are in disparate parts of England and finding it impossible to meet since both have indispensable business, taking them elsewhere. There is so much to be thrashed out, properties, annuities, bequests, the rents from her father's collieries and his own, though he is discreet enough not to mention the fact that he is in debt for £30,000, and the sale of Newstead once again in jeopardy because of Mr Claughton's defection.

His delays to her are becoming 'too like a dream' and she compares him to the procrastinating Hamlet. Still there are his letters to sustain her. He recalls his first sighting of her in the morning room at Lady Melbourne's, singling her out, her beauty, her deportment, her innocence, she 'no common being' but a luminary in that world of giddy and affected waltzers. Yes, she is to be 'the wife of his bosom', his whole heart will be hers, she his guide, his philosopher, his friend. She rides to the blacksmith's cottage to receive his letters and read them away from the prying eyes of her mother and the doting solicitude of her father. In the blacksmith's cottage she finds comfort in the fact that country people, as penetrating as any craniologist, have remarked that 'Miss' looks as if she has been a wife these twenty years, inferring a high ideal of conjugal felicity. A woman whom she did not know asked who might be 'the bonnie lad who [was] to tak awa the canny hinny'.

Except that the 'bonnie lad' was still in the Albany alone as he said with his menagerie of birds; his morning routine a bout of sparring with his boxing master, then posing in Albanian costume for Thomas Philips, the portrait painter, his only female companion being Mrs Mule. He omitted to mention the visits of Miss Eliza Francis, another putative author who believed that an audience with Byron would inspire her. She herself left a record of these trysts, all was sunshine, except for rats scurrying about, Byron starting from his chair, holding out both hands to her, as she ventured to ascertain the colour of his eyes. Then she reeled in shock, almost fainting because Byron had to put his arm around her waist, lifted some little curls that had escaped from under her cap, kissed her and clenched her to his bosom with an ardour which terrified her.

The engagement to Annabella had engendered piquant interest, was announced in the Durham paper, then contradicted in the *Morning Chronicle*, a petty malice that Byron believed to be the work of Caro, who had vowed that if Byron should marry, she would buy a pistol and shoot herself in front of the happy couple. She did however send him a letter laden with blessings, while telling John Murray that Byron would not 'pull' with a woman who went to church regularly and had a bad figure. Annabella it seems consumed large quantities of mutton chops and scones faithfully made for her by her father, but Byron was ignorant of any gluttony, having only met her twice. Colonel Leigh, who cannot have been blind to his wife's adoration of her half-brother, tolerated it because of Byron bailing them out again and again. Leigh opened a book at Newmarket, taking bets as to whether the marriage would or would not take place. Secretly he was opposed to it since it would mean that Augusta would be the loser in Byron's fortune.

Patience at Seaham was being sorely tried. Lord Wentworth, Annabella's uncle and whose presumptive heir she was, had travelled especially from Leicestershire to meet the illustrious groom, only to be disappointed and leaving in a huff. Augusta was enlisted by Byron to write to Annabella, to 'soothe' her for his being provokingly detained in London. Annabella, so liking the countenance of this letter, persuaded her parents to invite Augusta also, in the hope that it would bestir Byron to set out. Augusta declined with a great semblance of regret. She was nurse to baby Medora, governess to her eldest girl and something of both to the two intermediate babes. She wrote most cloyingly to this person she hoped soon to call 'sister' and already loved as such.

Annabella's desperation was increasingly evident in her letters and her craven plea as she relayed Lady Judith's directions for Byron's epic journey north – 'After you come to Boroughbridge, the nearest way hither is by the following stages, Thirsk, Tontine Inn, Stockton, Castle Eden, *Seaham*', imagining, as she said, that he was already there.

The nerves of their first meeting were preying upon her, yet she was certain they would prove to be admirable philosophers, remaining coolest in manner, though not cool within. Byron, also 'tremblingly alive' to that meeting, announced that he would be bringing Fletcher, his valet, but spare her the nuisance of a servant. From Six Mile Bottom, which he had made his 'inn', his feelings took a radical downward swerve and writing to Lady Melbourne, he said 'I am proceeding very slowly . . . I shall not stay above a week . . . I am in very ill humour.' He spent the next night at an inn in Wansford near Peterborough, arriving at dusk on 2 November, two days later than the fractious parents and his flustered 'intended' had expected him.

Annabella preserved the moment for posterity –

> I was sitting in my room when I heard the carriage, I put out the candles and deliberated what should be done. We met alone. He was in the drawing room standing by the chimneypiece. He did not move forward as I approached him, but took my extended hand and kissed it. After a while, he said in a low voice, 'It is a long time since we met.'

Feeling overpowered she left the room to call her parents. Yet he rallied at dinner, listened to Sir Ralph's stockpile of jokes, familially known as 'pothooks', jokes about fleas and frogs and electioneering and a shoulder of mutton. Lady Judith noted his excessive vanity, fiddling with his gold watch as he expounded on theatre matters, and she was appalled at his not having brought a gift or the customary diamond loop engagement ring.

That night, Mrs Clermont, Annabella's lady's maid and Byron's future nemesis, said that Her Ladyship was in tears as she undressed her. Byron told Lady Melbourne his fiancée was overrun with feelings, nothing but fine feelings and scruples and to crown it all, was taken ill every three days. He had grave doubts if marriage would come of it at all, as there was very little laughter and this boded ill for a man whose motto was 'giggle and make giggle'. But the die, as he said, was cast, the lawyers had met, the marriage settlement was afoot and neither party could now secede.

Annabella, to his alarm, made a scene, not very different from one of Caro's, at which he turned green and fainted away. He had been hinting at some mysterious shadow in his past and cited the wrong she had done him by rejecting his earlier proposal, something he would wreak revenge for. She decided to call off the engagement, sensing some awful impediment, and it was at that moment he fainted and she knelt in remorse at his feet. Some forty years later, she described the incident to Harriet Beecher Stowe, for though her whole life in narratives, letters and disquisitions was spent in self-vindication, she wished the world to know that Byron had loved her. She would conceal from the world her humiliation at his having so easily seduced her.

At her bidding Byron left sooner than intended, because being under the same roof and not married proved a strain on her nerves. At Boroughbridge, we find him once again in gallant mode. 'My Heart,' he wrote, 'we are thus far separated, but after all one mile is as bad as a thousand', fuelling the fiction that once they were married, their differences would evaporate.

FIFTEEN

Wedding plans and wedding bells were, by his reckoning, in 'a pestilent fuss'. The cake had been made at Seaham and he hoped that it would not go mouldy. Sir Ralph had penned an epithalamium, one verse so farcical, as Annabella said, she had to rewrite it. Her letters to Byron have become craven – 'mine mine . . . ever thine . . . I hope for a line from you today . . . I cannot enjoy anything without you . . . those long black days'.

Byron had applied to the Archbishop of Canterbury for a special licence, so as to be married anywhere, anytime and without fuss. Bridegroom and his best man Hobhouse set out on Christmas Eve, Hobhouse dispatched to Cambridge while Byron made a detour to Six Mile Bottom, for his last rending hours with Augusta, thwarted somewhat at finding that Colonel Leigh was actually at home. On Christmas Day, with the thermometer way below freezing, he writes to Annabella wishing her 'much merriment and mince pye'. It was Augusta who had to persuade him to set out on Boxing Day, Hobhouse noting that never was lover in less haste.

When the two men arrive at Seaham late on 30 December the mood is one of gloom and disquiet. Lady Judith has taken to her bed and Annabella, as Hobhouse saw, 'so doatingly fond' of Byron, she threw her arms around him and burst into tears. He also noted that she was dowdy-looking in her long high dress, but that 'her feet and ankles [were] excellent'. Next day the papers were signed, a mock marriage was performed, with Hobhouse standing in for Annabella, to familiarise the clergyman, the Reverend Thomas Noel, Lord Wentworth's illegitimate son, with the proper procedure. The evening dinner was conducted with a strained merriment.

On the morning of 2 January 1815, Byron in full dress paced the garden, the Reverend Noel, clerically clothed, sat silent at the breakfast table, Lady Judith so jittery she could not pour tea. Kneelers borrowed from the church were set down in the alcove of the bay window in the first-floor drawing room as the 22-year-old bride was being dressed by Mrs Clermont. Just before eleven o'clock, Annabella descended the stairs on her father's arm, wearing a white muslin gown trimmed with lace and a muslin jacket. Reciting the wedding vows, Annabella seemed to Hobhouse to be firm as a rock, Byron, as he later claimed, 'saw nothing, heard nothing' and while saying the vows, albeit stumblingly, a mist seemed to float before his eyes and he recalled his first sweetheart Mary Chaworth and their parting in a room at Annesley.

Afterwards, Lady Judith gave her son-in-law a tepid kiss, then to his annoyance there was a rowdy carillon of bells from the nearby Saxon church, muskets were fired and local miners in pantaloons enacted a version of a sword dance in which the fool figure was beheaded. Hobhouse presented Annabella with a set of Byron's poems bound in Moroccan leather, wishing her many years of happiness. With a naïveté, she said if she were not happy it would be her own fault.

Then of his friend Byron, Hobhouse took 'a melancholy leave'.

Melancholy and worse characterised the forty-mile journey to Halnaby, another of the Milbanke houses, in Yorkshire, which Sir Ralph had loaned them for their honeymoon. Snow and rain outside and inside the carriage an eruption. Bare of all reason and even sanity, Byron embarked on a singing spree, then turned on her, saying he was a devil and that he would prove it, that he had committed crimes which she, for all her catechising, could not redeem him of and that she would pay for the insult of having refused him two years earlier. Moreover, her dowry was a pittance. At Durham, as joy bells rang out to honour their passing, the execration grew worse, presaging the three bizarre, unhinging weeks that in his blither moments he referred to as 'the treacle moon'.

Their arrival has the suspense and thrall of gothic fiction – a sprawling mansion, a fall of snow, servants holding lit tapers, noting that the bride looked listless and frightened and that her husband did not help her down from the carriage. And so began the most public marriage of any poet, so infamous in its time that it was lampooned in *John Bull* magazine and the subject of endless scrutiny, helped by the confessions of Byron himself in his Memoirs, as Tom Moore recalled it, and by Lady Byron's numerous and increasingly incriminating testaments to her lawyers and afterwards for her own 'Histoire'. Though professing to Moore a reluctance to 'profane the chaste mysteries of the Hymen', Byron, according to Moore, 'had Lady Byron on the sofa before dinner'.

His tenets regarding the sleeping arrangements were categoric. Enquiring if she meant to sleep with him, he claimed to have an aversion to sleeping with any woman, but that she could if she wished, one animal being the same as the next, provided it was young. She who in her charter for a suitable husband had recoiled from insanity was to have her fill of it. Their wedding night has its literary correlation in the works of Edgar Allan Poe, a crimson curtain catching fire, a hallucinating bridegroom believing he was in hell, then pacing the long ghostly gallery with his loaded pistols.

By morning Annabella would say that 'the deadliest chill' had fallen upon her heart. By morning also she was to conceive of her first suspicion of Augusta, 'transient as lightning, but no less blasting'. Meeting her in the library, Byron waved a letter from Augusta in which she had addressed him as 'Dearest first and best of all human beings'. Augusta described being clairvoyantly at one with his agitation at the precise moment that the marriage vows were exchanged in Seaham, likening it to a sea trembling when the earth quakes. The letter, as Annabella noted, affected him strangely and sent him 'into a kind of fierce and exulting transport'. Augusta's spectre stalked Halnaby and breaking down in front of her maid Mrs Minns, Annabella said that she feared something dreadful had formerly happened between brother and sister. There would be many portents, such as a chance remark of hers on Dryden's *Don Sebastian*, the story of a sinning brother and sister, sending him into a violent rage as he took up his dagger, which was on the table next to his loaded pistols, and disappearing to the gallery that adjoined his bedroom. In those black moods he hinted at unspeakable crimes that preyed upon him, saying he already had fathered two natural children and that they were fools to have married. He then set about her re-education, telling her that right and wrong were merely conventional phrases. Morality was one thing in Constantinople and quite another in Durham or London. Yet his letters to the outside world were filled with his customary banter; to Lady Melbourne, not 'waxing confidential' any more, he said that Bell and he got on extremely well and so far she had not bored him.

His moods would run the whole gamut from taunts to savagery, to hallucination and even to momentary contriteness when he said she should have a softer pillow than his heart to rest on, and she retaliating by asking whose heart would break first, his or hers. She describes the tears that would suffuse his eyes, then freezing there and giving the appearance of icy hardness. Soon she is writing to Augusta, her one solace, craven letters, asking that this sister-in-law be 'her only friend' and the crooked reply, 'Oh yes I will indeed be your only friend.' Augusta's letters to her 'dearest sis' are masterpieces of ambivalence. Annabella is deemed the most sagacious person to have discovered the art of bringing B back to good humour and giggles and when Annabella, in glaring contradiction to her reserved nature, admits to her tireless enthusiasm for sex, even when menstruating, Augusta retaliates with a rapier thrust – 'I'm glad B's spirit does not decrease with the moon. I rather suspect he rejoices at the discovery of your ruling passion for mischiefs in private.' Smarting at receiving no 'scribbles' from Byron himself, she justifies it by listing his many occupations, walking, dining and playing at drafts etc., while warning Annabella to keep him away from the brandy bottle, an injunction that was in vain.

Before returning to London, Byron decided *he* would visit Six Mile Bottom, encouraging Bell to stay with her parents or go on to London, something she bridled at, what with her suspicions aroused.

When she crossed the threshold of that 'most inconvenient

dwelling', she was to step into a sexual labyrinth. Augusta came from upstairs, her ringlets carefully coiled, and while in her letters sisterly sentiment had brimmed over, she shook Annabella's hand 'in a manner sedate and guarded', then embraced Byron, who was in great perturbation. With Colonel Leigh being absent, the couple were bequeathed the marital bedroom!

'We can amuse ourselves without you, my charmer' Annabella was told after supper, as Byron dispatched her to bed and so initiated the hideous game in which she would lie awake each night listening to their laughter in the room below and then hours later, his 'terrible step' as he arrived to bed drunk, swearing at Fletcher, who had the job of undressing him, then taunting her, 'Now I have *her*, you will find I can do without you as well in all ways.'

The fifteen days that followed were enough to send any young woman, let alone a bride who had scarcely left the cocoon of her family, into the throes of hysteria, but Annabella kept her composure, this self-command driving Byron to worse furies. In the evenings, flush with brandy, he conducted his cruel pantomimes, his 'facon de Parler' as Augusta preferred to call them. She would be ordered to read aloud copies of the letters he had sent her, charting his courtship of Annabella, hollow and treacherous epistles, as they now proved to be. Yet Guss complied because Goose must not be driven to a tantrum or worse, a silent rage in which he might even stab himself. Lying on the sofa he insisted that both women embrace him so that he could then, in the grossest language, compare their ardour. He wrote to Hobhouse that he was 'working both women well', his own perfidy not dilated upon, except to add that it was tumblers of brandy at night and magnesia in the morning.

There were no confrontations, no showdowns, each playing her or his part in this macabre ritual. Just as Byron had lied to himself during the courtship, a lie that he was now exacting vengeance for, Annabella would construct her own edifice of lies. She was present, as she would later testify in Beeby's shorthand to her father's lawyers, when Byron rose at dawn and went across to Augusta's room, she was made barbarously aware of Augusta refusing him during her menstruation, and Byron alluding to it with 'So you wouldn't, Guss' and returning to make gross professions of desire to her. Yet she never questioned. She saw that brother and sister brazenly wore identical gold brooches with locks of their hair and crosses that signified consummation, but she rationalised, equivocated, convinced herself that Augusta was a victim just as she herself was, that both were instruments of his brutishness. She even told herself that although Augusta submitted to his affections, 'she never appeared gratified by them'. On their walks together Augusta, however, gave her no encouragement, Byron perhaps did not love her, but with perseverance and habit, to which he was susceptible, she might win over his affections.

The presence of children did not seem to intrude at all on the various and infernal parlour games, but according to Ethel Mayne, Annabella's biographer, Byron did once point to Medora and say 'You know that is my child', then went on to calculate the time of Colonel Leigh's absence from the family home, proving that it could not be the husband's.

It was Augusta, ultimately, who instigated their departure, Byron reluctant to leave and as his wife noted, waving his handkerchief passionately, straining for a last glimpse; then sinking down beside her, he asked her what she thought of the other A.

To Tom Moore he was proud to announce that Bell was showing 'gestatery symptoms' but for her part, Annabella in her commonplace book wrote, 'My heart is withered away, so that I forget my bread.'

SIXTEEN

When Byron and Annabella moved into 13 Piccadilly Terrace, a house rented from the Duchess of Devonshire, Byron's two burning objectives were deliverance from that marriage and funds to go abroad. In a letter to Hobhouse while on his honeymoon, appealing to him to 'fix' on the useless Mr Hanson, Byron outlined his financial ruin –

> Newstead *must* be sold without delay – and even at a loss ... my debts can hardly be less than thirty thousand – there is six thousand charged to a Mr Sawbridge – a thousand to Mrs Byron at Nottingham – a Jew debt of which the interest must be more than the principal – another Jew debt ... a good deal of tradesmen ... a loan of sixteen hundred pounds to Hodgson – a thousand pounds to 'bold Webster' ... three thousand to George Leigh ... necessities – luxuries – fooleries and money to whores and fiddlers.

Annabella's dowry proved more theoretical than actual, as the main inheritance would come only at the death of her uncle Lord Wentworth, but Byron feared the said Baronet was eternal, the Viscount was immortal and both men were cutting a second set of teeth. The thousand pounds per year,

£700 for him and £300 for her towards her pin money, merely covered the rent. Then there were horses, a carriage and coachman, numerous servants, drinking, gaming and his box at Drury Lane Theatre to which Annabella was not invited. He had begun to dress completely in black, to emphasise both his ravaged spirit and the nobility of his lineage. Meeting with Walter Scott in John Murray's office, the older author was struck by Byron's noble character and melancholy vein. The two men swapped gifts, though the dagger, mounted on gold, which Scott gave him, was hardly ideal for a man who kept a sword and loaded pistols beside his bed, Fletcher having the onerous task of ensuring that they were not used. Byron's return gift to Scott was a large funerary urn in silver, filled with bones and bearing an inscription from Juvenal.

For a while, all the outside niceties were maintained. Annabella, in her white satin, paid her 'wedding visits', was a guest at Queen Charlotte's 'teas' and shown off to his influential friends, politicians, poets and bankers. To her father she wrote arch descriptions of their visits, the salmon not quite fresh, the sheep's wool still on the mutton fat, amiability masking the 'varnish of vice'.

His letters to friends closed with a customary flourish – 'Lady Byron is very well and desires her compliments . . .' – but indoors a gothic nightmare was unfolding, her air of virtue, her sense of infallibility, her incarnate conscience were driving him mad and eventually, as he would tell Hobhouse, he felt himself to be 'bereaved of reason'. What servants would witness in Piccadilly Terrace hardly befitted the actions of a peer, Byron wrecking furniture, grinding his gold watch to pieces, then flinging it in the ashes, determined to spread misery on all those around him, but especially on his wife.

Augusta's visit in April, which he warned Annabella against, exacerbated the tensions. Intimacy, baby talk and late-night canoodling between brother and sister were resumed and in Annabella's graphic account of it one wishes that she had taken the path of a poet and not been given to liturgical epistles – 'I used to lay awake watching for that footstep by which my hopes and fears were decided . . . it was always expressive of the mood that had the ascendancy. It was either the stride of passion, which seemed to print its traces on the ground with terrific energy', or the animal spirits and laughter that confirmed his satisfaction. Pacing in the room above and charged by 'the continual excitement of horrible ideas', the thought crossed her mind to pick up one of Byron's daggers and plunge it through her rival's heart. After a stay of two months, Augusta was asked to leave.

The 'sweets and sours' of married life was how she had described things in the early and tolerable months, but as things worsened she had to suppress her jealousy and throw herself at the mercy of Augusta, 'her only friend', asking how long more she could bear it. Bailiffs had installed themselves in the downstairs hall, poised to repossess their furniture, Byron's library and the very beds they slept on. According to Annabella, one of the bailiffs became 'the subject of her husband's romance', upon learning that he had camped in the house of Richard Brinsley Sheridan for an entire year. Annabella wrote wretchedly to her father about their distressing circumstances, but Sir Ralph wrote back to say he could not raise mortgages on his properties and had narrowly missed jail himself. The hue of opulence was going, as was the hue of her hopes. In a poem that she wrote at that time, she describes her husband's tread at which she used to rejoice now filling her with mortal fear.

Yet to others, at that very same time, Byron could summon all his old gallantry and generosity of spirit. When Mr Murray learnt that Byron was obliged to sell his library because of his increased expenses and the new mode of his life, he sent a letter with an enclosure of £1,500 and the assurance that another sum of that same amount should be at his service in a few weeks. Byron replied almost immediately –

> I return your bills not accepted, but certain not *unhonoured*. Your present offer is a favour which I would accept from you, if I accepted such from any man. Had such been my intention, I can assure you I would have asked you fairly, and as freely as you would give; and I cannot say more of my confidence or your conduct.
>
> The circumstances which induce me to part with my books, though sufficiently, are not *immediately* pressing. I have made up my mind to them and there's an end.
>
> Had I been disposed to trespass on your kindness in this way, it would have been before now, but I am not sorry to have an opportunity of declining it, as it sets my opinion of you, and indeed of human nature, in a different light from that in which I have been accustomed to consider it.

But for Annabella the situation was becoming more hideous and she told herself that his treatment of her was due to his being temporarily mad. She would consult medical journals to diagnose his condition and secretly met with Dr Baillie, who had known Byron since his Harrow days, to talk of any earlier telling symptoms. Subsequently she consulted her own physician, Francis Le Mann, and with her governess Mrs Clermont, whom Byron loathed, watched for signs of his escalating eccentricities. When they saw that he took to lowering his head, then gazing from under his eyebrows, they saw it as resembling the King's caprices before his descent into madness.

It was said of Byron that he had never let imagination usurp the place of reason, but in those few months before her accouchement his reason failed him, his hatred of Annabella spiralling, describing her as 'a nice little sullen nucleus of concentrated savageness'. The situation became so unbearable that she invited Augusta to be with her, deciding now that he loved and hated them together. The end of the marriage might in Goethe's estimate be 'poetical and in keeping with Byron's genius', but to those in Piccadilly Terrace it was inexorable nightmare; the servants including Fletcher in terror and Augusta no longer able to restrain him, had to ask their cousin Captain George Byron to come as their protector.

Annabella and Augusta were both pregnant, swollen bodies which Byron loathed, comparing them with the sylph-like figure of his mistress, the actress Susan Boyce, whom he was threatening to bring to live under the same roof. In the last week of Annabella's confinement, Byron said that he hoped that both mother and infant would die and as she went into labour he left for the theatre. Returning at a late hour he sat in the room beneath, striking the necks of soda water bottles with the butt of his pistol, the impact of the glass pinging on the ceiling as Annabella laboured in the room above. On 10 December 1815, 'the winged creature' that he had imagined as being a son was a daughter, and looking at her his first words were said to be 'Oh! What an implement of torture I have acquired in you'.

But it was for Annabella that his greatest tortures were reserved. Two days later he burst into her bedroom, dismissed the servants and locking the door, he insisted on his conjugal rights, the dark and deviant demands evidenced in sworn statements to her lawyer, speaking of his untoward abuse of her, and the subsequent legalistic warning – 'A woman has no right to complain if her husband does not beat or confine her – and you will *remember* that I have neither *beaten* nor *confined* you. I have never done an act that would bring me under the law – at least on this side of the water.'

On 6 January 1816 Annabella received her ultimatum from him in a letter delivered by Augusta – 'When you are disposed to leave London it would be convenient that a day should be fixed and if possible not a very remote one for that purpose. Of my opinion upon that subject you are sufficiently in possession and of the circumstances which have led to it, as also to my plans or rather intentions for the future.' Bowing to his authority, she replied the next morning, 'I shall obey your wishes and fix the earliest day that circumstances will admit for leaving London.' Very early on the morning of 15 January, with her maid and the infant Augusta Ada, the carriage already waiting, she left the house. Passing Byron's bedroom, she noted the large mat on which his Newfoundland dog was to lie and for a moment was tempted to throw herself on it and await all hazards, but it was only for a moment.

Surprisingly, she wrote two friendly letters on the journey to Kirkby Mallory in Leicestershire, where her parents now resided, since the demise of Lord Wentworth. She hoped that he was remembering her medical prayers and injunctions and not giving himself up to what he had called 'the abominable trade of versifying' and refraining from the brandy. From Kirkby, she addressed him as 'dearest duck', saying that both her father and mother were eager to have the family party completed and that there was 'a sulking room' to which he could retire. Later she would say that she had written these letters on medical advice and that it was not to revive 'diseased associations' with him. Within twenty days she would metamorphose from accommodating wife to avenging Fury, as the quotidian nightmare of her marriage was brought home to her. Ann Rood, her maid and the future Mrs Fletcher, described her riding her horse wildly along the sands to 'stun her sconce' and at other times gave a picture of her rolling around the floor of her bedroom in paroxysms of grief. Meanwhile, in Piccadilly Terrace, Dr Le Mann could discover nothing like 'settled lunacy' in Byron, irritability yes, weeping, the shakes, spells of grandiosity, pains in the hip, pains in the loins, a torpid liver, but not settled lunacy. Augusta was 'in an agony of nerves', receiving irate summonses from her *sposo* to come home, trying to restrain Byron from drinking with Hobhouse, whom she wished dead, and most of all wishing for Annabella's return in order to avoid the shocking revelations that were bound to ensue.

Lady Judith wore her nightcap to dinner because the pressure of her wig was too great as she set about the rigorous interrogation of her daughter and was to hear, with hesitation, the ordeal of the thirteen months. Having consulted a young lawyer, Stephen Lushington, she hurried to London, bringing with her a memo written by Annabella, documenting some of the wrongs and grievances she had endured. From Mivart's Hotel she enlisted the services of Sir Samuel Romilly, a barrister in Chancery, whom Byron called a monster of perfidy, and even in exile, hearing of Romilly's suicide, hoped that in his annihilation he felt a portion of the pain he had inflicted on others. The Milbanke team of litigants would prove to be jackals in comparison with Byron's dilatory and more anarchic crew. When Stephen Lushington suggested to

Hanson that he should interrogate his client a little more stringently with regard to the several accusations against him, Hanson foolishly replied that Byron's memories were 'very treacherous'.

On 29 January, a letter addressed to Byron from Sir Ralph, drafted by Lushington, was delivered to Piccadilly Terrace. Augusta, guessing its contents, returned it unopened to Annabella, saying that for once in her life she ventured to act according to her own judgement, warning of a host of evils if Annabella did not return. When Byron himself finally received the letter a few days later, he was, as Hobhouse said, 'completely knocked up by it': 'Circumstances have come to my knowledge which convince me that with your opinions, it cannot tend to your happiness to continue to live with Lady Byron. I am yet more forcibly convinced that her return to you after her dismissal from your house and the treatment she experienced while in it is not consistent with her comfort, or, I regret to add, personal safety.' Sir Ralph proposed that each party should appoint a lawyer to discuss the terms of separation. Byron fumed. Replying haughtily, he said that as to the vague and general charges against him, he was at a loss to answer them and would anyhow confine himself to the tangible fact, which was that Sir Ralph's daughter was his wife, the mother of his child, and it was with her he would communicate.

He spent hours in his room, the doors locked, firing his pistols intermittently and writing a slew of letters to Annabella that veered from affectionate to righteous to desperate. He admitted to his phases of gloom, to his 'deviations from calm', but assured her that he would not be parted from her without her express and expressed refusal, their hearts still belonged to one another and she had only to say so and like Petruchio he would 'buckler his Kate against a million'. The twenty days since she left, had, as he said, poisoned her better feelings, but with each passing day those poisons would be magnified. Annabella was compiling her deadly narrative, which would make him regret the boast of sticking to tangible facts.

Annabella herself was soon installed in Mivart's Hotel, having brought her commodious memoranda to show to Stephen Lushington. When she told him of her suspicion of an incestuous relationship between Byron and Augusta, Lushington was at first too shocked to believe it, but mindful of her undeviating rectitude, he then did believe it but said it could not be raised in the separation wrangle, because she as a wife was barred from giving evidence and the charge could not be proved. He advised that they should stay narrowly within the bounds and cite 'brutally indecent conduct and language'.

But the 'great gulph' was widening and Byron began to falter. He begged her to see him and when she refused, Augusta went as his advocate to Mivart's Hotel, finding 'a woman pale as ashes, her voice quite altered, yet manifesting a deathlike calm'. She also saw that Annabella was resolute and would not be swayed. Byron's friends were alarmed by the rumours that began to circulate, escalating day by day and garlanded with both salacious and criminal accusations. When Kinnaird told Hobhouse of the homosexual charges, Hobhouse quaked at the very word and in his diary denoted it with a dash.

So it was a round of letters, pleadings, rancour, gossip, betrayals, accusations, Byron hitting on the bizarre idea that he could sue those who were estranging him from his wife and when that failed, following with a childlike plea: 'Dearest

Pip, I wish you would make it up, for I am dreadfully sick of all this', except that Dearest Pip was on her crusade of retribution. Caroline Lamb, the 'villainous intriguante', asked for a meeting with Annabella, saying she had secrets to tell, that if Byron were merely menaced with them, he would tremble and capitulate. They met at night and Annabella took minutes of the conversation in which she was told that her wicked husband had admitted to corrupting his page, Robert Rushton, and that he had perverted three young boys at Harrow. Worse, Caro produced copies of intimate letters that Augusta had written to Byron and that he had treacherously passed on to her. Annabella brought this new incriminating evidence to Lushington, who congratulated her on her lucky escape from the contamination of Byron.

The tide had indeed turned, vials of wrath poured upon him from high and low, Lady Melbourne's letter brief but merciless: 'I cannot see you at home' was followed with a perfunctory note to Hobhouse requesting that all her correspondence to Byron be burnt. Mary Godfrey, writing to Tom Moore, said 'The world are loud against him and vote him a worthless profligate' and so it was. In the Tory newspapers he was likened to Henry VIII, George III, Nero, Caligula and Epicurus. Byron teetered between outrage and self-aggrandisement, his name, which had been a knightly and noble one since his forefathers had helped to conquer England for William the Norman, was being 'tainted'. Stephen Lushington, ever assiduous, had learnt that Susan Boyce was dismissed from Drury Lane Theatre because of having contracted syphilis from him, and another actress, Mrs Mardyn, who barely knew him, was dismissed because a cartoon had depicted them cavorting. Byron was advised by Hobhouse not to go to the theatre lest he be hissed at, nor to

Parliament, yet Byron paid a visit which he knew would be regarded as abhorrent.

It was to a glittering gathering of Lady Jersey's, the reigning beauty and hostess of the period, that Byron went in April, bringing Augusta, eight months pregnant, with him. Disbelief at his audacity was soon followed by the scurrying feet, the shocked enamelled faces of the ladies frozen in indignation and the men refusing to shake the hand of this 'second Caligula'. The black and blighting calumnies were no longer mere speculation, all London knew of the dawn flight of his wife of one year with her infant daughter, of the diabolical fact of his relationship with his half-sister, affirmed by Byron's own imprudent boasting of it and worst, the repugnant crime which could not be spoken, which could scarcely be whispered, the sodomising of his wife, a sin that could not be mentioned among Christians. Only Lady Jersey and a skittish young heiress, Miss Mercer Elphinstone, spoke to Byron, Miss Elphinstone chiding him for not having married her. Byron leant upon the chimneypiece and stared back at the room, silent, adjudicating and contemptuous. Why they went remains a mystery, considering that Byron had described Lady Jersey as 'the veriest tyrant that ever governed Fashion's fools', but why they stayed is at once a testament to his pride and the lonely leave-taking of the world he longed to be accepted in.

As the wrangling and menaces between the lawyers continued, Byron knew that worst crime with which he could be charged and even likened himself to the sodomite Jacopo Rusticucci in Dante's Seventh Circle of Hell who, because of his shrewish wife, succumbed to the errors of sodomy; but he also knew that his own shrewish wife and her team of jackals, terrified of lurid public opinion, would not dare bring the charge to an open court and that for all their threats, the only expedient would be a private separation. Hobhouse, still, though somewhat comically, mindful of Byron's reputation, advised that he get a disclaimer from Lady Byron, disavowing cruelty, systematic unremitting neglect, gross and repeated infidelities, incest and so on. Annabella did send the memorandum, but what she disavowed was her accusation of those dire deeds and not the acts themselves. As Byron waited for the separation papers to be signed, Augusta paid her last visit on Easter Sunday morning, bringing as a gift a Bible, which Byron would keep until his death. She was going home to Six Mile Bottom to give birth to her fifth child and guessing that they would not meet again, Byron wept uncontrollably and when she had gone wrote his bitterest letter ever to Annabella: 'I have just parted from Augusta – almost the last being you had left me to part with – & the only unshattered tie of my existence – wherever I may go – and I am going far – you and I can never meet again in this world – nor in the next . . . if any accident occurs to me – be kind to *her*.'

On 21 April the separation papers were finally signed, the carriage that had been their wedding coach he bequeathed to his wife, wishing her a more propitious journey in it, and the wedding ring, though of no lapidary value, containing the hair of a king and ancestor, he wished preserved for Ada, whom he referred to as Miss Byron. In the muddy matter of finances, he was the loser, having to agree to arbitration on Kirkby Mallory upon the death of Lady Milbanke, something he did not see as being very imminent.

Piccadilly Terrace was like a sacked house, his library and furniture having been sold, only a few faithful servants and his animals. Nightly visits from Hobhouse and Kinnaird sometimes ended in drunken brawls, Byron challenging his friends to a duel. It is astonishing that in such frenzied circumstances, Byron should have found another perch for his heart to alight upon. He began to be besieged with letters from a young lady who signed herself Jane, Clara, Clare and eventually Claire Clairmont and whose command of English contrasted greatly with the stilted and obfuscating language of the law. How refreshing for him to be asked: 'If a woman whose reputation has yet remained unstained, if without either guardian or husband to control her she should throw herself upon your mercy, if with a beating heart she should confess the love she had borne you for many years ... could you betray her, or would you be silent as the grave?' Byron did not answer at first, but when she begged to be admitted alone to meet him and in the utmost privacy, so as to gain advice on a theatrical career, he relented. Aged seventeen, somewhat buxom, she did not have the antelope looks that he was drawn towards, yet he was intrigued by her flashing intelligence and the fact that her stepsister Mary Godwin lived with Shelley, who was one of his avowed admirers. What he did not know then was that Shelley was also open to Claire's electrical charms and had christened her his 'little comet'.

Her next letter to him had some of Caroline Lamb's audacity. She suggested that they go out of town, some twelve miles or so, by stage or mail, to a quiet place where they were not known, she offering that which had been the passionate wish of her heart to give him. Whether they went out of town or met in London, ten minutes of happy passion, as she put it, would discompose the rest of her life.

In his book *The Love Affairs of Lord Byron*, Francis Gribble paints a scenario of Byron hounded, 'his household Gods shivering around him and the world training its hose of virtuous indignation upon him'. Byron put it more bluntly –

'I was unfit for England . . . England was unfit for me.'

Though financially mired, he prepared for exile like a nobleman. He appropriated the name Noel from the Milbanke family, following the death of Annabella's uncle, so that the carriage made by a Mr Baxter bore the initials NB and the coach itself was copied from one the Emperor Napoleon had seized at Cenappe. His retinue included a Swiss named Berger, Fletcher, the loyal but truculent valet, Robert Rushton, no longer his lover, now relegated to cleaning his armoury, and a private physician, Dr Polidori ('Polly Dolly'), a putative author, who before leaving England had secured from John Murray the sum of £500, to write a diary of the forthcoming eventful journey.

Hardly had they left Piccadilly Terrace when the bailiffs arrived, finding nothing to seize except the servants' fripperies, some squawking birds and a scabby monkey.

At the Ship Inn in Dover where the party, which included Hobhouse and Scrope Davies, had taken lodgings, great quantities of French wine were consumed, while they suffered a reading of an atrocious play by Polly Dolly and local ladies disguised as chambermaids came to gape at the notorious Lord. Earlier in the evening he had gone to visit the grave of a satirist, Charles Churchill, and in some funerary symbolism had lain down on it and later paid the verger a crown to have it returfed.

Early next morning, as the vessel set out on a rough sea with a hard wind, Byron stood on deck and raised his cap in farewell to Hobhouse, who ran to the end of the pier showering blessings on the friend of such gallant and kind spirit. He would never see England again.

In the sixteen-hour journey crossing the Channel, while his companions yielded to seasickness, Byron resolved to seize the themes that had been occupying him in those last frightful weeks. He began Canto Three of *Childe Harold*, of which Sir Walter Scott would say that it mirrored the genius of a powerful and ruined mind, like a shattered castle with its sorcerers and wild demons.

When the steamer arrived at Ostend at midnight, the restraints and detractions of England behind him, a great surge of creativity upon him, he felt such an exhilaration that when they arrived at the Coeur Impérial Hotel, much to Polidori's dismay, Byron fell 'upon the chambermaid like a thunderbolt'.

SEVENTEEN

'I breathe lead' he said, at last recognising that by losing Augusta, his sweet sis, the only selfless love he had known, the rock of his hopes and of his life had foundered. In the lyric 'The Castled Crag of Drachenfels', which he sent her along with some lilies of the valley, the poet celebrates the earthly paradise that he had lived with her, lamenting its loss and imploring her soul to come to his:

> But one thing want these banks of Rhine –
> Thy gentle hand to clasp in mine!

Later on, as he crossed the Alps on horseback and mules, the scenery beautiful as a dream, glistening peaks, crevices, storms, crashing avalanches, he enjoined her to love him, as she was beloved by him. He did have to confess to the 'interlude' with Claire Clairmont, asking her not to scold him, saying a foolish girl had come after him and he was fain to take a little love by way of novelty. What he did not tell her was that Claire was pregnant and had gone home to England 'in order to people that most desolate isle'.

Since leaving England, he had been adding verses on scraps of paper for Canto Three of *Childe Harold*; as he wrote to Tom

Moore, he was 'half mad during the time of its composition, between metaphysics, mountains, lakes, love inextinguishable, thoughts unutterable and the nightmare of [his] own delinquencies'. But his grief was no longer merely subjective, it was assimilated into the greater and irreparable tragedy of war. In May 1816, derouted to Brussels on account of the stately carriage breaking down, Byron paid a visit to the fields of Waterloo, with Polidori and an acquaintance from childhood, Major Pryse Lockhart Gordon.

That fluke when a writer chances on a situation, whereby the sluice gates of the unconscious are thrown open, is seismic. Waterloo was for Byron what the madeleine was for Proust. Ploughed fields, unmarked graves, importune boys selling swords, helmets, buttons and cockades, and yet standing there and in the next days returning to gallop over it was an apotheosis. In a note to Hobhouse he wrote how he 'detest[ed] the cause and the victors' and yet Waterloo wrung from him his greatest poem, contrasting the gaiety of the Duchess of Richmond's ball in Brussels with the cannons' opening roar and the eight-hour battle in which fifty thousand lives would be lost – 'Rider and horse, – friend, foe, – in one red burial blent!' It shows Byron at his most profound, signalling the horror of war, the pity of war and above all, the madness of war. In this he was akin to Goya, who at that very same time was painting his greatest, most searing and indignant canvases, depicting the battlefields where the Spanish militia and Napoleon's soldiers had inflicted such barbarities on each other.

But while Byron was brought face to face with the gravity of history, Augusta stood on less hallowed turf at home. Children with colds and chilblains, Augusta Charlotte showing signs of retardedness, Georgina having fidgets and

Medora still in the nursery, Colonel Leigh bilious and with a belated suspicion of her intimacy with Byron. Their debts were so exorbitant that they were endeavouring, but without success, to sell Six Mile Bottom to one Reverend William Pugh, only to find that though they owned the house, they did not own the paddocks in front of it. Her reputation almost in shreds, Augusta knew that her post as Lady of the Bedchamber to the Queen and the small stipend that came with it, were in jeopardy.

Byron did love her, was haunted by memories of her, that summoned trees and brooks and flowers, but he could also summon the Promethean strength that propelled him into poetry, whereas Augusta could not. Aeneas loved Dido and he trembled when her shade reached him far out at sea, yet he went on to great conquests, whereas Dido impaled herself on the sword that she had taken from him. Augusta did not impale herself, but what she did was to throw herself on the mercy of Annabella, who had joined an evangelical sect and whose prime motive now, with the collusion of Theresa Villiers, was to establish Augusta's criminality. She wanted from Augusta an admission of the irreparable damage she had done to Byron, a confession to the crime of incest. 'Do not suppose that I wish to exact any confession,' Annabella wrote, but that was exactly what she resolved to do. However, Augusta did not utterly crumble under these interrogations and in a hasty scrawl she protested her innocence: 'Dearest A, I have not wronged you, I have not abused your generosity . . . intentionally I have never injured you.' Annabella, now assigned as 'Guardian Angel', went on to tell her that she must relinquish the pernicious hope of ever seeing Byron again or of being his friend. How quashed Augusta must have been to learn that Byron had betrayed her by showing the babbling letters she had written him to two of her greatest enemies, Caroline Lamb and Lady Melbourne. Her pyrrhic victory was to send Annabella copies of the letters she was receiving from Byron, leaving the outraged wife to declare to Mrs Villiers, 'They are absolute love letters.'

Unaware of these conspirings, Byron continued to send Augusta gifts, crystals, jewellery, toys for her children and for Ada, along with humorous vignettes of his adventures: the imperial calèche breaking down again and again, the deroute to Brussels, the visit to the fields of Waterloo, pastured rich with the blood of the dead; music and waltzing in Brientz, Flanders a place of pavements, Cologne with a repository containing the bones of eleven thousand virgins and Verona housing the supposed tomb of Juliet. In Milan he was fêted as successor to Petrarch, where he also met the shy young Stendhal and was enraptured at being able to read the love letters and verses between Lucrezia Borgia and her uncle Cardinal Bembo, in the Ambrosian library. 'And beauty draws us with a single hair' he wrote, because of their shared affinity for Pope, promising to bribe the curator to let him take a strand of Lucrezia's hair to send to her.

He had written for Augusta a journal of the Alps, the '*Jungfrau* with all her glaciers; then the Dent d'Argent, shining like truth; then the Little Giant (the *Kleine Eigher*), and the Great Giant (the *Grosse Eigher*); and last, not least, the Wetterhorn', yet reminding her that neither these, the music of the shepherd, the crashing of the avalanche, nor glacier nor cloud lifted the weight upon his heart. In 'Stanzas to Augusta' she is referred to as the 'solitary star', the 'gentle flame' by which he is buffeted against total destruction. But it is *Manfred*, a three-act drama, begun in

Switzerland and completed in Italy, that is the most naked admission of his love of her.

'A very wild, metaphysical and inexplicable thing' as he said, inspired by the vastness of the Alps, Goethe's *Faustus*, and fuelled with the lava of his rage, regret and vengeance. Astarte, named after a pagan goddess, is the sister whom Manfred loved but his embraces were fatal to her. Alone in his Gothic castle in the high Alps, he summons the magical deities to grant him obliteration. Instead, Astarte appears but is numb to his agonised pleadings and vanishes as he endeavours to embrace her, at which he swoons. His battles continue on those cold heights, his suicide thwarted by a chamois hunter who gives him the wine of life, the spirits and the Witch of the Alps mocking him as a creature convulsed with passions and seeking things beyond mortality. With Promethean determination he wrestles with these supernatural forces, including the Giant Steed Death, vowing that 'his torture be tributary to his will', and in death he speaks defiantly to an abbot – 'Old man! 'tis not so difficult to die.'

Goethe might praise *Manfred*'s 'heavenly hue of words', but in England the repercussions were vicious and once more the gossip regarding his incestuous relationship circulated. When it appeared in 1817, it was savaged. *The Day* and *New Times* reported that 'Manfred has exiled himself from society . . . he has committed incest . . . Lord Byron has coloured *Manfred* with his own personal features.' Mrs Villiers, in a letter to Annabella, claimed never to have been so disgusted, so horrified, and that by its publication Byron must surely be damned in the eyes of the world. The indictment of Annabella herself, who appears as the 'other woman', with 'cold breast and serpent smile', could hardly have escaped her. Yet to Augusta

Annabella wrote imperiously, telling her how she must reply to Byron regarding this pernicious work – 'You can only speak of *Manfred* with the most decided expression of your disapprobation. He practically gives you away and implies you were guilty *after* marriage.' Augusta did write to Byron, but true to what Annabella would call her 'glissant' character, the disapprobation was muffled.

Augusta's replies to Byron's letters became more and more evasive, 'full of megrims and mysteries', so infuriating him that he asked her to rise above 'commonplace people and topics', except that she was the prisoner of commonplace people and topics.

From Venice, in 1819, he wrote Augusta a letter that must stand as the deepest testament of his feelings –

> My dearest Love – I have been negligent in not writing, but what can I say. Three years absence – & the total change of scene and habit make such a difference – that we have now nothing in common but our affections & our relationship. – But I have never ceased nor can cease to feel for a moment that perfect & boundless attachment which bound & binds me to you – which renders me utterly incapable of *real* love for any other human being – what could they be to me after *you*? . . . we may have been very wrong – but I repent of nothing except that cursed marriage – & your refusing to continue to love me as you had loved me – I can neither forget nor *quite forgive* you for that precious piece of reformation – but I can never be other than I have been – and whenever I love anything it is because it reminds me in some way or other of yourself.

She sent it to Annabella with a categoric request: 'Burn it.' Annabella did not burn it, she copied it for the lifelong 'Histoire' of the man she had spent thirteen months with and returned it to Augusta with a semblance of grace that had long deserted her.

EIGHTEEN

In November 1816, on a foggy night, Byron entered Venice, 'the greenest isle of [his] imagination', the black knots of the gondolas in the canal more beautiful to him than a sunrise, the fairy city of the heart in which he embarked on a spree of licentiousness. Everything about it was to his liking, the gloomy gaiety of the gondolas, the silence of the city, beauty inseparable from decay, and soon carnival, masquerade, balls and whores. Within four days he had secured a gondola, stabled his horses on the Lido, found an apartment close to St Mark's Square and enrolled in the monastery on the island of San Lazzaro, to take lessons in Armenian, his mind in need of something craggy 'to torture [himself] into action'. He had also fallen in love with Marianna Segati, the wife of his landlord. 'Pretty as an antelope, with large black oriental eyes, glossy hair, the voice of a lute, graces worthy of the Songs of Solomon' and the naïveté which he always found pleasing in a woman, which is how he described her to John Murray, adding that no twenty-four hours passed without 'giving and receiving unequivocal proofs of mutual contentment'. Byron's letters to Murray are unique in the exchange between publisher and author; authors write about their angst, their families, their impecuniousness, but hardly the intimacies of the boudoir.

Marianna's nemesis came in the person of another fiery young woman, Margarita Cogni, the *Fornarina*, wife of a baker, also young, with tantalising black eyes, the Venetian looks and the spirit of a tigress. Murray would be told in gleeful detail of the contretemps between these two women, La Segati and her gossips discovering by the neighing of his horse that he had gone late at night to meet the *Fornarina*, whence they followed, staging an operatic brawl, screams, curses, the throwing back of veils and in explicit Venetian, the *Fornarina* telling his *amica*: 'You are not his wife, I am not his wife, you are his Donna, I am his Donna', then stormed off. She then made herself indispensable to him in the running of the Palazzo Mocenigo, former home of the Doges, which he had rented for £200 a year, the *Fornarina* walking about in hat and feathers and a gown with a tail, intercepting his mail, paying a scribe to write letters for her, and servants continually 'redding the fray' between her and any other feminine persons who visited. Her Medea traits and Venetian 'pantaloonery' amused him for a time, but when she became ungovernable and he asked her to leave, she refused, wielding a knife, Fletcher had to disarm her. Boatmen carried her out whence she presently threw herself in the canal and was brought back intending to 'refix' herself in the palace. Byron threatened that if she did not quit the premises then he would, and ultimately she was returned to her irate husband.

The nineteenth-century watercolour by W.L. Price depicts Byron in his *piano nobile*, reclining on a chaise longue, with his dog at his feet, but there are other less languorous glimpses of that eccentric ménage. Shelley gives a hilarious account:

> Lord B's establishment consists, besides servants, of ten horses, eight enormous dogs, three monkeys, five cats, an eagle, a crow and a falcon; and all these, except the horses, walk about the house which every now and then resounds with their unarbitrated quarrels as if they were masters of it . . . later I find that my enumeration of the animals in this Circean palace was defective, I have just met on the grand staircase five peacocks, two guinea hens, and an Egyptian crane.

Shelley had been introduced to Byron by Claire Clairmont in Geneva in 1816 and both he and Mary were instantly captivated, but by the time they met again in Venice the friendship was fractured. They were appalled by Byron's debaucheries, consorting with the most ignorant, the most disgusting, the most bigoted and the most filthy creatures, Byron bargaining with mothers and fathers for their daughters, brazenly naming his conquests from contessas to cobblers' wives and claiming to have 'tooled' with two hundred women of one sort or another. But worse for them was his wilful and gratuitous cruelty to Claire and his cavalier treatment of the little daughter Allegra, who had come with her Swiss nurse Élise to live in the Palazzo Mocenigo, Byron's welcome less than fatherly, when in a note to Hobhouse he wrote: 'My bastard came three days ago – healthy – noisy – & capricious.'

When Claire's daughter was born in England on 12 January 1817, Shelley wrote to Byron to say 'the little being' was extremely beautiful, with the deepest blue eyes, and they had given her the name Alba, meaning dawn. After a year, following Shelley's enquiries about his plans for the child, Byron decided to 'acknowledge and breed her' himself. He gave her the surname Biron, to distinguish her from Ada, his 'little Legitimacy', and rechristened her Allegra. His conditions were that her mother would have no say whatsoever in the child's 'personal, moral and doctrinal education'. Claire conceded, because she was young, penniless and at first led herself to believe that Allegra would have a more privileged upbringing with her father, never foreseeing the tragic and peripatetic fate of the child.

'I have sent you my child because I love her too well to keep her,' Claire wrote aged twenty, having decided despite her misgivings to give the little girl up to Byron, believing that she would be guaranteed a brilliant future and not end up as a waif. From the moment the child was brought to the Palazzo Mocenigo by Mary Shelley's Swiss nurse, Claire was eclipsed. Allegra was pretty and precocious, but as Byron said, possessed of 'a devil of a spirit'. Claire would write asking for news. 'Do not make the world dark to me as if my Allegra was dead' she pleaded. He maintained his silence, and was caught up in the general dissolution of his life and entanglements with women.

Claire never saw the child again, even though she begged Byron to show mercy and at least be acknowledged as her mother, but she well knew that any word from her mouth was 'serpents and toads to him'. She wrote reams of letters, pleading, menacing, reproving and heartbroken, but they were ignored. His monstrous cruelty was both to punish the young woman who had brazenly pursued him and for whom he had formed such an antipathy, and to compound his own convoluted guilt.

When the 'adorable bambino' began to show the burning temperament of her father and her mother, Byron placed her in the care of the British Consul-General Richard Belgrave Hoppner and his wife, who was not particularly fond of her, and when they had to leave Venice she was entrusted to their servant Antonio and then transferred to Mrs Masters, wife of the Danish Consul, by which time she showed the remoteness of an abandoned child.

All Venice came to know the *stravagante* Lord, his black crimes written on his brow, stories of him jumping fully dressed at night into the canal, to seek out chance pleasures, carrying a torch to enable him to sight the oars of the gondoliers. The palace, as Byron conceded, was a 'bacchante with pieces to perish in', but insisted that there were no feelings, all was 'fuff-fuff and passades', and the women, by their own wiles or that of their mothers, extracted from him large sums of money and jewellery. England would be apprised of his harlotry, in a joint letter to Hobhouse and Douglas Kinnaird he recited the names –

> the Tarruscelli – the Da Mosti – the Spineda – the Lotti – the Rizzato – the Eleanora – the Carlotta – the Giulietta – the Alvisi – the Zambieri – the Eleanora da Bezzi – (who was the King of Naples's Gioacchino's mistress – at least, one of them) the Theresina of Mazzurati – the Glettenheimer – & her Sister – the Luiga & her mother – the Fornaretta – the Santa – the Caligari – the Portiera – the Bolognese figurante – the Tentora and her sister – cum multis aliis? & some of them are Countesses – & some of them Cobblers wives – some noble – some middling – some low – & all whores.

As his Rake's Progress continued, he suffered bouts of giddiness, 'flying rheumatism', syphilis, gonorrhoea and self-disgust, yet surprisingly found time to write, even though composition, as he told Murray, was akin to defecation and to him a great pain. George Steiner has noted that Venice was to Byron what Rome was for Corneille, a liberation, where 'the wing stroke of his imagination' flowered. He wrote with the spirit of the bull when penned, a sport which entailed some good tossing and goring. *Beppo*, an 'experiment in comic poetry', was written in 1817, depicting Venice as the 'seat of dissolution'. The story, concerning the plight of a lady happily ensconced with a lover and surprised by the reappearance of her husband, whom she believed lost at sea, was relayed to him by the husband of one of his mistresses. Racy and protean, it was as well 'full of politics and ferocity' and a precursor of his master work *Don Juan*, which Shelley predicted would be the greatest poem in the English language since Milton's *Paradise Lost*. How greatly it differed from the sensibility of his rivals, Shelley's 'silver music', Coleridge's 'wings of healing', Wordsworth's 'wild unpeopled hills' and above all from Keats, for whom Byron's greatest venom was reserved, challenging Keats's principles of poetry and his inordinate self-love. Keats, for his part, in *The Fall of Hyperion*, deems Byron a mock lyricist and 'careless Hectorer given to proud bad verse'.

The two hundred and twenty-two stanzas of Canto One of *Don Juan* were sent to John Murray with the claim that it was meant to be quietly facetious about everything. Quiet it was not, but blasphemous and bawdy, shot with indignation and a dazzling erudition, the high romance steeped in history and resonating with the influences of the

Old Testament, Virgil and Homer. 'Donny Johnny', as he liked to call his hero, 'sent to the devil somewhat ere his time', was indeed derived from Tirso de Molina's *El Burlador de Sevilla*, but his peregrination differs greatly from that of Molina's and from Mozart's *Don Giovanni*.

The 'scoundrel' Poet Laureate Robert Southey, to whom it was mockingly dedicated, was described as a 'warbler', a careerist and 'a dry Bob', a reference to his impotence; and Lord Castlereagh, former Lieutenant Governor of Ireland, an 'intellectual eunuch', steeped in Ireland's gore. It is a satire on man's Fall interwoven with Juan's fall from sexual innocence. The ideal love for Haïdée, daughter of a pirate, is destroyed as Juan is sold into slavery and Haïdée, with her unborn child, dispatched to an early grave. The subjective pathos is set brilliantly against the larger cosmic catastrophes and ordeals. Juan witnesses the dehumanising effect of battle and shipwreck, the lust of those who peddle in war, suffers the embraces of rapacious empresses and ultimately delivers his savage indictment of the English society he moved in before being cast out. This boundless universe of love, ambition, cupidity, war and cannibalism all rendered with a throwaway ease, Byron sometimes asking his readers to furnish an opinion of what they had read. 'Negligently great' is how Anne Barton describes it and Virginia Woolf would marvel at the 'elasticity of form' allowing of such freedom so that everything and anything could be included. Augusta, merely hearing of it, said that if it were persisted with, it would be the ruin of him.

As the 'rugged rhinoceros' John Murray received the cantos he was appalled; proposing cuts, omissions, suggesting asterisks for the more flagrant lines and summoning his synod, which included Hobhouse and Douglas Kinnaird. They railed at the barbarities, the indelicacies, the savage indictment of friends and acquaintances, but for Byron their imaginations were 'mere dunghills'. His remaining 'rags of patience' were cast off and he determined to battle his way like a porcupine, telling Murray that by such prudery he must also object to the works of Ariosto, La Fontaine and Shakespeare. He would not decimate. He would not mutilate.

If the poem was to be continued it must be in his own way as Murray was informed '– you might as well make Hamlet (or Diggory) "act mad" in a strait waistcoat – as trammel my buffoonery – if I am to be a buffoon – their gestures and my thoughts would only be pitiably absurd – and ludicrously constrained. Why Man the Soul of such writing is it's licence?' The delineation of Annabella as Donna Inez, mother of Don Juan, 'each eye a sermon and her brow a homily', was too near the bone, as was his cold compassionless view of humanity. Too much the delineation of shipwrecked sailors, killing, then devouring a dog, too much a picture of English nobles who voted, dined, drank, gamed and whored, their 'frolic ladies' doing exactly the same thing but with a great aptitude for deceit. An epidemic of disgust struck England, Hobhouse, Kinnaird, Samuel Rogers, Tom Moore, conceding to its brilliance, but saying that it must not be published and Augusta, who had not even read it, predicting that it would be the ruin of him.

Don Juan was published anonymously on 15 July 1819, but there was never any doubt as to who was its author. Keats, it is said, threw the work away in disgust on his way to Rome and Wordsworth predicted it would do more harm to the English character than anything of that time. The couplet which Keats and others took such exception to concerned survivors in a longboat who had lost their comrades in a shipwreck, their grief however secondary to the pangs of hunger in their bellies:

> They grieved for those who perished with the cutter,
> And also for the biscuit casks and butter.

Byron flinched at nothing, his view of humanity remorseless, his outlook radical. War was 'a brain-spattering, windpipe-slitting art', mercenary soldiers were butchers and other soldiers recruited on half pay, merely there to satisfy the war-mongering egos of their generals, from which Wellington was not exempt.

As with all of his work, it was not the poetry itself that would be reviewed but the man. *Blackwood's Edinburgh Magazine* thought it an infernal work, 'a filthy and impious poem' whose offences speak the wilful and determined spite of an 'unrepenting, unsoftened, smiling, sarcastic, joyous sinner, brutally fiendish, inexpiably mean'. But Byron would not be silenced and Murray quaked as new and even more incriminating verses reached him.

Byron seethed with creativity yet found it inadequate to soothe the rage and restlessness within and so the round of pleasure and debauch continued, the several women having no name at all, but comprising one vast, female, gargantuan vortex. Then a surprising transformation, his falling in love at the very instant when he had decided to turn away from it.

Where English bile and publishers' pusillanimousness had failed with regard to *Don Juan*, the entreaties of this muse-to-be succeeded. Countess Guiccioli had read a pirated French translation of cantos of the poem and found it 'abominable', wresting from Byron the promise that he would not continue with it. His blood 'all meridian', his heart likewise, he agreed, or as he put it in a letter to Hobhouse, 'As I am docile, I yielded.'

NINETEEN

On 2 April 1819, Countess Teresa Guiccioli, coming into a fashionable salon in Venice, realised that her destiny was sealed by the sight of the 'celestial apparition' sitting on a sofa. The apparition was Byron, who in slight sulk had placed himself, along with his friend Alexander Scott, on the sofa, opposite the entrance, determined not to mingle. It was at Countess Benzoni's weekly *conversazione* that the Countess, a vivacious woman of sixty, who was rumoured to have been one of Byron's conquests, asked him to meet the young woman who had just arrived with her husband Count Alessandro Guiccioli. Teresa, three months pregnant at the time, was in mourning for the deaths of her mother, one of her sisters and an infant that had only survived four days. Byron was reluctant, saying he did not wish to meet any more women, ugly or beautiful. But Scott and the Countess prevailed upon him and crossing the room he was introduced to Teresa as 'Peer of England and its greatest poet'. In her *Vie de Lord Byron* written long after, she wrote that she had been captivated by the melody of his voice and the smile which Coleridge had also likened to 'the opening of the gate of Heaven'.

Hearing that she was from Ravenna, Byron's interest quickened because Ravenna was 'a poetical place', since it housed the tomb and monument of Dante and Francesca da Rimini. So while invoking the names of Petrarch and Dante, the flame was lit and Teresa recalled that when she left that room with her husband, she was already shaken to her soul.

Count Guiccioli, proud, acquisitive and manic, forty years her senior, was something of a satyr, suspected of two assassinations, thought to have poisoned his first wife Contessa Zinanni, whose great wealth compensated for the disparity of their ages and her physical imperfections. He also begot six children by their maid Angelica, whom he later married, her death leaving him free to propose to Teresa Gamba, daughter of a Count Ruggero from an ancient Romagna family. Six months out of a convent, Teresa would later say that she had been 'sold' into marriage by the importunity of her mother and others, but to her future husband she wrote effusive letters, adding kisses that she would not send to a brother. He was 'her adorable husband' and now Byron was to become her adorable *cicisbeo*, the *cavaliere servente* that every married woman in Italy believed herself entitled to.

At their first encounter, they spoke of Dante and Petrarch and the following day a boatman ferried her to Byron's gondola and then to a private 'casino' where the constraints of mourning were soon forgotten. Before a week has passed she is calling him *Mio Byron*, disdaining all discretion in the salons and publicly affirming her claims on him. The Count maintained his customary aloofness, but he did advance the day of their departure, to one of their villas on the Po, causing Teresa such agitation that she sought out Byron in his box at the opera, during a performance of Rossini's *Otello*. As Teresa would write later, in that 'atmosphere of melody and harmonious passion' she broke the news to him and was helped into her gondola by both husband and lover, deriving courage 'from the silence and the starlight'. One of her preliminaries, as he told Hobhouse, was that Byron must promise never to leave Italy. He had no intention of leaving Italy, but he did not choose to be frittered down into a regular *cicisbeo*, except that he already was. To her he was writing: 'Everything depends on you, my life, my honour, my love. To love you is my crossing of the Rubicon and has already decided my fate.'

She was gone, with a husband, violently sensual, to whom she still was in thraldom, providing that whetstone of jealousy and uncertainty that maddens lovers. Venice now became 'sea Sodom', he had tired of promiscuous concubinage and Ravenna was where he was going, but wishing first to be 'sure' of her and not to be a laughing-stock. His blood 'all meridian', he was in no doubt that this wild and headlong passion was fraught with danger and uncertainty. She consumes his thoughts as he pictures her, a princess, beyond the Mountains, walking by the banks of the River Po, whereas he, alone and unsure, is a mere Stranger of the land.

Meanwhile in Ravenna, she is struck down with a mysterious illness, swoons, has a consumptive cough, her only consolation being that sometimes her spirit skims over the Venetian lagoon to be with him. They found intermediaries for these bulletins to be passed in secrecy; Fanny Silvestrini, another histrionic woman and Teresa's former governess, dispatched Byron's epistles, while Padre Spinelli, a former priest, was waiting to receive them and deliver them in secret to Teresa at the Palazzo Guiccioli.

Byron set out on 1 June 1819, across the Veneto, passing through Padua and stopping at Ferrara, where a particular inscription, *Implora Pace*, on a tombstone in the Certosa Cemetery struck him as being fitting for his own tombstone, not wishing, as he wrote to John Murray, to be 'pickled' and sent home.

Teresa's instructions to him along the way become vague and contradictory, these vacillations unnerving him, so much so that from Padua he is writing to Hoppner: 'I am proceeding in no very good humour – for La Guiccioli's instructions are rather calculated to produce an éclat and perhaps a scene.' He insinuated that the 'Charmer' should have been less liberal with her favours in Venice.

It was on that broiling journey, which he likened to 'conscription', that he completed the beautiful lyric, 'Stanzas to the Po', enshrining Teresa as a 'lady of the land', but unable to conceal how utterly he had succumbed.

> The Slave again, Oh Love! at least of thee!
> 'Tis vain to struggle, I have struggled long
> To love again no more as once I loved.
> Oh! Time! why leave this earliest Passion strong?
> To tear a heart which pants to be unmoved?

However, his ardour was somewhat challenged by a letter from Teresa after he arrived in Bologna and felt 'like a sausage'. She proposed a different plan for their meeting, as the Count had surprised her by suggesting that they move to another of his estates at a moment's notice. He was now the weary and waiting suitor, having to suffer the hospitality and drearying anecdotes of the local nobles, debating with himself whether he should continue on his journey or return to Venice.

Teresa's illness proved to have been a miscarriage and briefly reverting to more satiric mode, Byron, in a letter to Douglas Kinnaird, said he was 'certes' that the foetus was not his. Hobhouse, who had been apprised of her charms, including her quick temper and her enigmatic heart, is warning him not to go after this 'terra firma' lady, but to keep with the Venetian naiads.

Two days later, bewildered and lovesick, he sets out for Ravenna, arriving on 10 June 1819, which was a holy day, pavements strewn with rose petals, streets covered in awnings, palaces draped with tapestries and brocades, all of which he took to be auspicious. He is installed in yet another cheerless inn, awaiting word from Teresa, who at that very same moment is writing to ask him to postpone his visit, as she has had a serious relapse and foresees difficulties at seeing him alone. She tempers his disappointment by saying that she does not feel she 'deserves' the attentions of one so noble as he.

But Byron having trudged so far is in no mood to return and writes to say he is entirely and eternally hers. Next day the Count pulls up outside the humble little inn in his coach-and-six, to fetch Byron to the palace. The bedside scene with Teresa flushed, fevered, coughing blood, a husband, a lover and a host of nervous relatives, merely heightened the operatic tableau.

Each day Byron is permitted two visits, Teresa and he rarely alone, relatives all too willing to take him to Dante's tomb, to the Byzantine mosaics in San Apollinare, to the library with Dante's manuscripts, except that his heart is too heavy for any sightseeing. Love has its martyrs and he is one of them, writing her letter after letter in the small stifling bedroom, sentiments not too different from those that the young coachman might be penning in his stable – if he loses her what will become of him – their few moments of happiness have cost too much, he is alone, completely alone, she once so dear, so pure, seems nothing now but a menacing and perfidious shadow. Preferring death to uncertainty, he asks her to elope with him, guessing as he put it that her reply would be 'divinely written' but would end in a negative, and so it did. Should he, he then asked, leave Ravenna? She dissimulated, her next letter a charming discourse on his poem *The Lament of Tasso*, curious as to what secret suffering had produced such beautiful lines and particularly wishing to know who was the origin and inspiration for the heroine Leonora.

With her courtesan's gifts for surprising him, Teresa rose from her sickbed, greeting him on the staircase, then stepping into his closed carriage for a drive to the *pineta* woods. The Count and entourage followed in a carriage behind. For the lovers there followed an idyllic interlude, the woods to which they rode each evening once a backdrop for Boccaccio's amours and now for them 'delicious, dangerous, ecstatic love'. Byron the poet and Teresa the would-be poet enshrined their memories of that place and that time.

In *Don Juan*, which he resumed a year later, he would recall the pines and thickets of the 'immemorial woods', his unsurpassed happiness at the twilight hour. Teresa gave her own heady version, their dismounting to sit under the resinous pines, the sweet smell of thyme and other herbs, lingering until the sounds of the vesper bells from the Duomo came faintly through the trees, when they would ride back, then part, certain to meet later on at the theatre or at a soirée.

Now that she was seen abroad his jealousy was further inflamed, not only was he jealous of the inscrutable husband, but of those men she acknowledged from her box at the opera:

'My thoughts cannot find rest in me ... I have noticed that every time I turned my head towards the stage you turned your eyes to look at that man ... but do not fear, tomorrow evening I shall leave the field clear to him. I have no strength to bear a fresh torment every day.' Teresa loved these declarations, wrote on the margins 'magnifique, passione, sublime', and kept them for her *Vie*, that histrionic and glorified record of their relationship. To Hobhouse, however, he was more despairing, saying his hair was half grey, admitting to a weariness and asking if he could trust the morrow. Augusta was told of his new conquest – 'She is pretty – a great coquette – extremely vain – excessively affected – clever enough – without the smallest principle – with a good deal of imagination and some passion.'

Gossip began to circulate, Mylord's reason for staying on in Ravenna was because of his hopeless love for the Countess and moreover, the time chosen for his calls on Teresa coincided exactly with the siesta hours of the husband. From Rome her young brother Count Pietro Gamba, who had been informed of Byron's courtship, wrote to say that he trembled for her peace, she whose heart was so pure and so noble, warning her against any intimate tie with a man so strange and of so doubtful a reputation, one who in spite of his rank was rumoured to have been a pirate in the East. Teresa's reply confirmed her indifference to strictures and her innate mettle:

> Why should I not love such a friend? The feelings I have vowed to him are stronger than all arguments and, in loving Lord Byron as I love him, I do not think that I am offending the holy laws of God. You ask me to give up this friendship, but why? Is it because of the Count? But it is his wish that Byron is here. Is it because of what the World will say? But

> this world whose acquaintance I have scarcely made, I have already appraised; I have realised its vanity, its injustice and its incapacity to fill a Heart and Soul that has any other than frivolous and vulgar needs.

Anonymous letters reached Count Guiccioli. Skittish verses portraying him as a cuckold were circulating along with mischievious tattle. At one grand gathering the women insisted that Byron was so beautiful, that their men should agree to have him exiled. Fearing the moment when they must be parted, Teresa had a relapse and managed to convince her husband that the doctors of Ravenna were not skilful enough, that she was only half cured and needed to go to Venice to consult with one Dr Aglietti, whom Byron had summoned to Ravenna earlier on and who had diagnosed her condition perfectly, prescribing leeches and Peruvian bark. The Count curiously gave his permission, saying she might travel with her maid and her manservant, Byron as 'her travelling companion' to follow in his own coach. From Venice, Teresa wrote daily to her husband swearing constancy, complaining of a little cough, a bad headache, piles, indignant at any suggestion that she might deceive him.

When the Count, along with his son by an earlier marriage and a train of servants, arrived unexpectedly at the Palazzo Mocenigo, all semblance of graciousness had gone. Determined to pluck out the worm that he believed was gnawing at her heart, he had prepared a document outlining her faults and misdemeanours. He had also a set of rules, essential to her future behaviour. She must not be late in rising, must not be fussy in lacing and washing, must busy herself in household matters, striving towards the greatest cleanliness, be prudent in spending, allowing time for reading and music, receiving as few visitors as possible, be docile with her husband, submitting her own views provided that they were sweet, modest and tentative. Teresa's reply was neither sweet, modest nor tentative. She asked to be given a horse with everything necessary for riding and to receive without discrimination any visitor who might come.

But the Count had a more insidious card to play, which was to appeal to Byron's sense of honour. The gossip and calumnies regarding the couple had reached Teresa's father, Count Ruggero Gamba, who requested that Byron should not return to Ravenna. Such a move, as Count Guiccioli pointed out, would not only create enmity between two noble scions, but it would bring shame on Teresa's five innocent sisters and ruin their prospects of marriage. Naturally, Teresa was not to be apprised of this tête-à-tête. Byron capitulated. Teresa rebelled, the Count cried on Byron's shoulder and the outcome was an unhappy couple returning to Ravenna and Byron sagely asking 'Could Love for ever/Run like a river . . .' The answer was no.

Since he could not be with her, he must leave Italy altogether. His friend Alexander Scott advised against it, quoting Machiavelli, saying that 'a prudent prince does not keep his word when to keep it is against his interests'. But leave he must. He prepared to vacate the palace, to dispose of its contents, had his horses and his gondola sold, intending to spend just a few weeks in England before moving on to South America. In London, he intended to fight a duel with the journalist Henry Brougham, who had savaged his *Hours of Idleness*, and naturally to discuss his ever complex finances with Mr Hanson and Douglas Kinnaird, including the investments from the Noel estate, which he shared jointly with Annabella. Little Allegra was to travel with him.

This news of his pending arrival almost gave Augusta a stroke. Upon hearing that he was shortly to be in Calais, she wrote for Annabella's advice and the reply was swift and categoric. Augusta must not see him, she being the principal object of his coming to England, in order to renew his 'criminal desires'.

Teresa, a captive in her husband's palazzo, was in the throes of grief and despair, believing that she was being deceived and that in fact Byron had ditched her. Fanny Silvestrini wrote reams to dissuade her of this, stressing Mylord's agony as he prepared to cross mountains and seas in a bitter season, all to spare her the torture of waiting and wondering if he would come to Ravenna. Puzzlingly, she added that should Teresa desire him ever to return from England, he would do so expressly for her sake. Byron, she reported, was a lonely man, refusing an invitation to the Benzonis' or any place of amusement. Teresa would have letters from Calais, from London, from wherever his lonely wandering took him.

With what Byron would call her 'usual sublimity', Fanny painted a picture of the fateful day –

> Byron was already dressed for the journey, his gloves and cap on, even his little cane in his hand. Nothing was now waited for but his coming downstairs – his boxes being already on board the gondola. At this moment Mylord, by way of pretext, declares that if it would strike one o'clock before everything was in order (his arms being the only thing not yet quite ready) he would not go that day. The hour strikes and he remains. Evidently he had not the heart to go.

Meanwhile, Teresa had suffered a serious relapse and was pleading with her distraught father to invite Byron to come and winter in Ravenna. So, with her father's goodwill and her husband's 'acquiescence', Byron was invited to return. Love had won.

TWENTY

With the daring of a 'Triton come ashore' is how Byron described himself on his second pilgrimage to Ravenna. Leaving Allegra in Venice he set out with his servants, not sure if it would be for a week or a lifetime. En route at Bologna he did something that can hardly be thought insignificant. After a haircut he had 'all his long hair' posted to Augusta as a keepsake. When he arrived at Albergo Imperiale in Ravenna on Christmas Eve 1819, in deep snow, he was given a rapturous welcome and before long would be recognised by papal legates, vice-legates and society as Teresa's '*serventissimo*'.

When news of his domestic situation reached England, Augusta thought it 'an insanity' and Hobhouse, conferring with Murray, deemed it 'bad news'.

It was carnival time in Ravenna, as it had once been in Venice, masks, disguises, flirtations, and in his excess of joy he claimed never to have seen such youth, such beauty, and more diamonds than were seen 'these fifty years in Sea-Sodom'.

Ravenna suited him, the citizens not so debauched as the Venetians, old Italian manners and customs everywhere in evidence, Dante's tomb, the little cupola more neat than solemn, a spur to future poetry. With his lady on his arm,

Byon attended the morning and evening rituals, tried his hand at mastering how to double a shawl and was occasionally rebuked by Teresa for a deficiency in the virility of his soul. He was happy to be in a remote part of Italy where 'no Englishman resided before' and he certainly took up a challenge that no Englishman in his right mind would have accepted. The Count invited him to rent the second floor of the Palazzo Guiccioli and so in February he sent for Allegra, left the Albergo Imperiale bringing all his furniture and his menagerie, which included cats, dogs, a monkey, a tame hawk and a guinea hen, placing himself under the Count's 'untiring espionage'.

For this, the Count had enlisted eighteen servants, an accountant, several maids, a carpenter and a locksmith, but as Byron blithely thought, 'love laughs at locksmiths'. Two blackamoors in embroidered costumes with daggers in their belts acted as rival go-betweens, one from New Guinea loyal to the Count and Luigi Morelli from East Africa loyal to Teresa.

There were lovers' quarrels, gossiping servants and impassioned letters between Byron and Teresa passed along the single staircase each hour, Teresa often complaining that he did not love her as intensely as before and Byron outraged at how she responded to her husband's doting words and glances, observing that as he sat by the fire reading, he could not be blind to the intimacies between them, she vilely complacent, as he put it, in her conjugal duties. Teresa conducted both amours with the deftness of a Borgia. She went secretly to Byron's rooms during the two hours after dinner when the Count rested, Morelli guarding the door. She enlisted a blacksmith to remove the lock to Byron's apartments because her husband had a second key, and discovering this treachery, the

Count had the new lock removed and replaced with another. It is surprising that, in the thick of all these intrigues and machinations, this 21-year-old woman kept her head and apparently her charms.

For twelve months the Count colluded in what Teresa would later call 'a tortuous game'. But all three were playing a game, Teresa flaunting Byron as her *amante*, while assuring her father Count Ruggero and her brother Count Pietro Gamba that the relationship with Byron was without stain, the Count venting his reptilian temper on her, yet greeting Byron with an enigmatic courtesy. Then one evening, returning prematurely from one of his estates, the Count surprised the lovers in what Byron called 'quasi in the fact'. Unlike Becky Sharp in *Vanity Fair*, protesting her innocence to a husband who had just discovered her in the arms of Lord Steyne, Teresa remained imperturbable. She was poised to succeed in her most unshaken endeavour, which was to make Byron commit to her and allow her to break with the scheming, sordid, avaricious and obstinate Count. Alone with him that night, the threats and intimidation were such that she wrote to her father the following morning asking to be allowed home and begging him to plead with the Pope to grant her a separation. True to her plucky nature, she asked why she should be the only woman in Ravenna not to be allowed a *cavaliere servente*. Her father, who had opposed the liaison with Byron, had his mind so drastically changed by Teresa's admission of the brutality she had had to endure, that he challenged Count Guiccioli to a duel.

Even the townspeople, who knew of the misdemeanours in the Palazzo Guiccioli, took Teresa's side, their rationale being that the Count had known all along of the relationship and had accepted it. Moreover, the fact that the Count had borrowed money from Byron and had even tried to use Teresa as his advocate to borrow several more thousands of His Lordship's guineas, not only tainted him but proved him to be somewhat of a pimp. The fact that he insisted on sleeping with his wife after her admission of faithlessness did not elevate him in people's eyes. All Ravenna seemed implicated in these cloak-and-dagger happenings, along with priests, cardinals and spying servants.

The Count was determined that a separation decree should not be granted. He did not want to lose Teresa or seem inferior in the eyes of his noble relatives and most of all, he did not want to pay back her dowry or give her the obligatory allowance of one hundred scudi a month. He tried several strategies, enlisted the papal legates at Ravenna, marshalled more spies, setting them on Byron not only as adulterer, but as a dangerous and subversive agent, who was an enemy of the Vatican.

After two months of suspense, in July 1820 Count Gamba received the Pope's decree, stating that it was 'no longer possible for her to live in peace and safety with her husband'. He sent it to Teresa, along with an edifying letter from Antonio Rusconi, Cardinal Legate of Ravenna.

> Most illustrious lady! [the Cardinal wrote] His Holiness having been informed that your Ladyship has found herself in circumstances in which she can no longer live in peace and safety with her Husband, Cav. Alessandro Guiccioli, His Holiness has benignly condescended to authorise me to permit you to leave your Husband's House and to return to the House of your Father, Count Ruggero Gamba; so that you may live there in such laudable manner as befits a respectable and noble Lady separated from her Husband.

> Further, the Holy Father, in order that Your Ladyship may not be deprived of the necessary provisions and all that is requisite for the noble and decorous state of a Lady, condescends to assign you one hundred scudi a month, which shall be paid by the Husband in such manner and means as the integrity and providence of the Holy Father directs and shall be conveyed to you in future by the Cardinal Legate, the present writer, in fulfilment of the Sovereign Command. Furthermore, it is the considered and express wish of the Holy Father that Your Ladyship, in leaving your Husband's house, shall take with her such linen, clothing and other objects as appertain to the decent adornment of a married Lady, as well as all that may be required for bed and board, following an inventory of these objects, to be signed by both parties, excepting valuables which your Ladyship did not bring with her to her Husband's House, and which she received as gifts on the occasion of her Wedding. The Cardinal Legate, in communicating these Sovereign decrees, consigns them with the truest and most distinguished esteem.

Teresa thanked Cardinal Rusconi, wishing for the honour to kiss his 'Holy Purple'. The Count was apprised of the letter by one of his spies and ordered that none of the horses be taken out of the stables that day. Bizarrely, at dinner, husband and wife maintained the customary etiquette, the Count serving her, talking pleasantries of this and that, when two hours later Morelli had succeeded in hiring a coach and with the help of Byron's cook, Teresa and her maid were whisked out of the house, and somewhere on that fifteen-mile stretch to Filetto, her father was waiting for her.

The separation, with the Pope's permitting it, was the first of its kind in Ravenna for two hundred years and constituted both a triumph and, for Byron, a liability. He well knew that in that society a woman separated from her husband on account of her lover was in a precarious position, the lover compelled by honour to marry her, except that for Lord Byron marriage was 'the graveyard of love'.

But he was and would be for three years 'dreadfully in love with her' and as he wrote on the index page of her copy of Madame de Staël's novel *Corinne*, Teresa 'comprised [his] existence then and hereafter'. For her part, she would claim that he wrote better in her presence, that he needed her voice and her chatter, being totally at one with her. The Gamba family, father, brother and younger sisters, were also to fall under Byron's spell, he making the fifteen-mile journey each evening on horseback to Casa Filetto, a seventeenth-century house set amongst olive groves, woodcock and partridges in the pine forests beyond, a setting for 'pastime and prodigality'.

It was there too that Byron's political fervour was reinvigorated, what with young Count Pietro talking 'wild about liberty' and Count Ruggero, a prominent member of an insurgent group committed to the liberation of the Romagna region from papal and Austrian rule, marshalling Byron to their cause. Theirs was a secret organisation known as the Carbonari, or charcoal burners, and had drawn recruits from patricians, liberals and malcontents who chafed at having to be subservient to the Austrians under Metternich.

In 1815, after the defeat of Napoleon, Italy was carved into several principalities and Ravenna fell under papal rule. Byron had always advocated his love of freedom, and what could be more inciting than an underground movement, intent on overthrowing papal authority, restoring Italy to the great and glorious reigns of Augustus and Julius Caesar? There were meetings in the Gamba house or out in the woods, warlike speeches, the odd assassination, slogans on walls, 'Long live the Republic' and 'Down with the Pope', Byron offering lavish sums of money along with his services as a volunteer. To his friends in England he wrote of a most interesting spectacle, the Italians, a race that he admired more than any on earth, determined to send the barbarians of all nations back to their own dens. Requesting swords and ammunition, he claimed that the rebels were going to fight the Huns and do savage work as Italian anger was on the boil. 'The very poetry of politics', as he put it.

Italy was to become a field of battle. Decisions were imminent and many a finger itching for the trigger. Americans had enrolled with the Carbonari and were 'on tiptoe to march'. He was made captain of a group called *La Turba*, or the mob, and though their numbers were a few hundred, he wrote to John Murray of them being in their thousands. He had ordered harnesses and portmanteaux for the horses. A fray had already begun at Russi, a town not far from Ravenna, assassinations at Cesena and in all, forty assassinations in the Romagna. While agog with all these happenings, he was dashing off notes to Murray concerning the controversy in England over Bowles and Pope, attending subversive dinners in the forest, drinking Imola wine and arranging a weekly pension for a 94-year-old woman, a wood gatherer, who rewarded him for his generosity with a bunch of wood violets.

The uprising was planned to take place in February 1820, but intelligence had reached the Austrians, who advanced a week earlier, crushing the Neapolitan Carbonari on the plain of Rieta.

The Ravenna contingent, learning of this massive defeat,

lost the incentive to rise and moreover, were intimidated by an encyclical issued from the Vatican, saying that they risked excommunication by belonging to such a subversive sect. The uprising petered out, the Carbonari lost heart and as Byron ironically put it, some even went hunting. Teresa wept by her harpsichord, said Italians would once more have to return to opera, Byron adding that it and macaroni were their fate. The aftermath for him was even more ludicrous. Two nights later, Count Pietro left a bag of bayonets, muskets and some hundreds of cartridges, turning his rooms in Casa Guiccioli into a 'depot' and but for Lega, a loyal servant, taking them in, Byron would have been in a 'scrape', as other servants would have betrayed him.

The flame of revolution quenched, Byron was once more driven from his public self to his private self and into that crater of melancholy that he dreaded. Teresa was to see the other Byron, the werewolf – 'As to my sadness – you know that it is in my character – particularly in certain seasons. It is truly a temperamental illness – which sometimes makes me fear the approach of madness – and for this reason, and at these times I keep away from everyone.'

Often in bad spirits, the weather dull and drooping, Byron 'scribbled and scribbled'. Teresa had rescinded her veto on *Don Juan*, so further cantos, 'with a proper mixture of siege, battle and adventure', were despatched to England to give Mr Murray jitters and Englishmen and women another dose of revulsion. Friction between him and Mr Murray had been mounting, Murray excoriated as 'an unnatural publisher' and 'a paper cannibal'. In Byron's eyes Murray would become 'stepmother' to the work, ashamed, afraid, negligent, even deciding not to put the publisher's name on the index page,

Byron reminding him that it would be a long time before he would 'publish a better poem'.

His decision not to take money for his work was long since gone. He now wished to be paid, and handsomely so, and when money matters seemed to drive a deeper wedge between them, Byron wrote saying 'mercantile matters' were 'better dealt with by [his] banker Douglas Kinnaird', adding that angry letters would hardly adorn 'their mutual archive'. As the pernicious effect of his work was felt in England, Byron quite sensibly exploded and asked, 'Who was ever altered by a poem?'

Along with *Don Juan*, he wrote verse dramas, drawing on ancient worlds, ranging from the picaresque to the plangent and the blasphemous. The first was *Marino Faliero* (1821), the story of a fourteenth-century Venetian Doge, who fought against corrupt rulers and had his head cut off for it, the only immortalising of him in the Doge gallery being a strip of black cloth in which he was deemed a criminal. Byron did not want it performed, yet despite Murray's efforts to get an injunction from the Lord Chamberlain, a cut version of the play was performed at Drury Lane Theatre in London. There followed in December 1821 *Sardanapalus*, a tragedy about the last King of Assyria, which was influenced by his re-reading of Seneca; and then *Cain*, in which Byron's unclean and subversive spirit once again scandalised England. Murray had advised against the satanic sentiments in it, a criticism which Byron chafed at, asking Murray did he wish Lucifer to sound like the Bishop of Lincoln? When Murray himself was in danger of prosecution for merely publishing it, gallantry was briefly restored, Byron swearing that such a disgraceful eventuality would bring him hurrying to England.

But bad temper kept resurfacing because of the many spiteful reactions to his works. An accusation of plagiarism in a critique of Canto Two of *Don Juan* appeared in *The Monthly Review*, Byron charged with having stolen the shipwreck scene from Sir J.G. Dalyell's *Shipwrecks and Disasters at Sea*, published in 1812. Though he claimed that it had made him laugh, he was incandescent with rage. His shipwreck scene had been inspired not by one single shipwreck but from all the actual accounts of them, including a journal by one of his ancestors, and he wished Murray and England to know that no writer had ever borrowed less from predecessors.

On 24 September 1821, while still in Ravenna, Byron wrote his most scalding and relentless letter to his publisher. It is a masterpiece of rage, reproach, self-righteousness and ultimately the epitaph of a wounded man whose country had cut him off. 'Dear Murray' it began,

> . . . I wish to propose the following articles for our future – That you shall send me soda powders – toothpaste – toothbrushes . . . that you shall *not* send me any modern or (as they are called) new publications in English – whatsoever – save and excepting writing, prose or verse, of Walter Scott – Crabbe – Moore – Campbell – Rogers – Gifford – Joanna Baillie – Irving (the American) Hogg-Wilson (Isle of Palms Man) or any especial single work of fancy which is thought to be of considerable merit.

The quantity of trash he had received as books was in his opinion incalculable and neither amused nor instructed him. Reviews and magazines were 'but ephemeral and superficial reading'. In Italy very little was known of literary England except what reached them 'through some garbled and brief extract in some miserable Gazette'. His closing words were even more haughty – 'I will keep my mind free and unbiased by all paltry and personal irritabilities of praise or censure ... to let my genius take its natural direction.'

TWENTY-ONE

'I am going to Pisa' Byron wrote to Augusta in October of that year, implying that things were different between him and Teresa, and in throwaway manner said, 'You know that all my loves grow crazy – and make scenes.'

The Gamba family, because of their imprudent revolutionary zeal, were banished from the Papal States, destined to permanent exile, seeking asylum in one place after another, stripped of their honour and whatever means they had had. Teresa refused and eventually only agreed after being told that by the orders from the Vatican, she would either be sent back to her husband or despatched to a convent.

Byron, 'not so furiously in love' as at first, did not follow with the alacrity that Teresa would have wished. Packing, preparing, swearing, sweating, blaspheming, setting out across the Apennines, over bad roads and torrential rivers, was not at all conducive to his work. Also, the news of his intended departure from Ravenna was deemed a public calamity, the poor sending petitions to the Cardinal in order to persuade Byron to stay.

'What are you doing, my Byron, what are you thinking?' Teresa wrote, adding that the two hours before sunset were an unbearable agony for her, fearing that he would be assassinated in the woods by either the Vatican spies or the Austrian police. Indifferent to such a fate, he wrote back to say he had misgivings about going, foreseeing very serious evils for the Gamba family and for her in particular. At other times he clung to the unlikely belief that he might be able to use his influence with Comte Giuseppe Alborghetti, Secretary General of the Province, who had the trust of the papal legate, to have the family pardoned and reinstated. The Mother Superior in the convent at nearby Bagnacavallo, to which he and Teresa had placed Allegra a year earlier because she proved 'obstinate as a mule and ravenous as a vulture', had heard a rumour that he was leaving Ravenna and wrote to invite him to pay a visit. She enclosed a letter of Allegra's: 'My dear Papa – it being fair time I should so much like a visit from my Papa as I have many desires to satisfy; will you please your Allegra who loves you so?' Byron found it lacking in flattery and merely a stunt to get 'paternal gingerbread'.

His procrastinations to Teresa were myriad, waiting for the post from England, an intermittent fever, a second application for permits as Lega, the buffoon, had let the others expire, carriers to be procured from Pisa for his furnishings, as those at Ravenna were too expensive. After two months a convoy set out with his saddles, his books and his bed on the long journey over the Apennines by Covigliaio, Pistoia and Pisana, but Byron still remained in the empty palace along with the servants, sleeping on straw beds and, as Lega was to tell Teresa, 'Mylord is in very ill humour.' His banker, Pellegrino Ghigi, was the unfortunate one to be donated most of Byron's animals, a goat with a broken leg, an ugly peasant dog, a bird of the heron type which only ate fish, a badger on a chain, two very old monkeys, and any transactions pertaining to Allegra's education.

With his aversion to scenery, he set out on 29 October in the dark hours before dawn, and on the road between Imola and Bologna, half asleep, his carriage met with another carrying Lord Clare, his friend from Harrow, and the meeting of a mere five minutes seemed to annihilate all the years between, filling him with a sweet sensation as if rising from the grave, claiming he could feel Lord Clare's heartbeats in his fingertips. On that same road further along his carriage passed a public coach, taking Claire Clairmont from Pisa to Florence to commence her duties as a governess, a last glimpse of the man she so vauntingly pursued and who had shattered her life.

The carts carrying his possessions had arrived ahead of him, the officials of the *Buongoverno*, alerted to the danger that he might be, had sent their reports to the Grand Duke. A student by the name of Guerazzi wrote that an extraordinary man had arrived in Pisa, 'one of royal blood, great wealth, sanguine temperament, fierce habits, masterly in knightly exercise and possessing evil genius'.

On the road between Florence and Pisa and in the spirit of atonement, he had written a 'versicle' for Teresa, which by being in English, she perhaps did not see that it lacked the aching sentiments of 'Stanzas to the Po', written for her some two years earlier.

Casa Lanfranchi, which the Shelleys had found for him, was a sixteenth-century feudal palazzo on the Arno, built of Carrara marble, which suited Byron's sense of grandeur, as did the hearsay that Michelangelo had designed the staircase. Spacious it was, though not with sufficient stables to house his eight horses, his imperial carriage and the three other carriages necessary for conveying the coterie of friends which Shelley had gathered in order to establish a 'utopian' circle in Pisa. Fletcher was also convinced that it housed ghosts, so that it replaced Newstead in Byron's gothic imaginings, Newstead, after so many long delays and bogus auctions, had been sold, much of the £94,000 it fetched swallowed by Byron's debts.

A translation of his poem *The Prophecy of Dante* had been submitted to the Commissioner of Pisa, who informed the Grand Duke that it would indeed 'augment popular agitation and encourage fanaticism in youths'. The translator had added his own hackneyed opinion of the work for the Duke's perusal – he had found it turgid, difficult to digest and had had to divest certain images of their prosaic garb, assuring the Commissioner that he had merely translated it to serve the Party. Circulation was promptly prohibited. Yet Byron carried on in his insouciant ways, sleeping till noon, having seltzer water and biscuits, then sometimes from sheer hunger downing a concoction of cold potatoes and fish with vinegar, to quell his appetite, but as he told Edward Trelawny, he had no palate. Trelawny, a Cornishman, dark with flashing eyes, the very epitome of a pirate, claimed to have slept with a copy of Byron's *Corsair* under his pillow and had come to Italy expressly to join Byron's circle. He would, in the fullness of time, vilify his benefactor and write a vicious memoir in which Byron was charged with a vacillating mind, self will, with being intolerant, peevish and vindictive, his apparent cordiality a fraud, his whole character contrasting vilely with Shelley's sublimity of soul.

Teresa had to be content with seeing her *cicisbeo* when he visited her and her family in the small villa, Casa Parra, on the Lung'Arno, because Byron had entered a gregarious phase among the medley of expatriates that included Shelley, his cousin Tom Medwin, Trelawny, Captain Williams and Walter Savage Landor, who on principle spoke to no Englishman except Byron. Medwin encouraged Byron to reminisce, slyly gathering material for a book, which he published after Byron's death and which Fletcher pronounced as containing 'no conversation of his Lord'. Later, Leigh Hunt, with his petulant wife and yahoo children, would be added to the circle, living on the ground floor of Casa Lanfranchi, Shelley having conceived the idea that they would launch a magazine, *The Liberal*, which Augusta, now sedulously pious, predicted to Annabella would be 'atheistical'. Hunt would also write a bilious and untruthful memoir of the man whom he troubled day after day, despite his 'sorriest arithmetic', for a cool hundred of his crowns. Byron, filled with avarice and cowardice, was in Hunt's opinion the consequence of an unhappy parentage and ought never to have existed.

Away from the Adriatic and unable to swim, Byron resumed his practice of marksmanship, only to discover when he applied to the Governor, from whom he could hardly expect leniency, that it was forbidden to carry or use firearms in the city. He rented a pasture from a farmer some few miles outside it, to which he and his boisterous friends repaired each afternoon, to compete with each other by shooting at silver coins wedged into forked sticks. When Teresa learnt that the farmer's daughter was being decked with armloads of very pretty bracelets, she decided that she and Captain Williams's wife Jane would ride there each day by coach to witness the boyish feats of their wanderlust men.

Byron gave lavish dinners with all the refinements of Regency England, his staff of eight supplemented with extra help, quicksilver conversation and gossip, which was not at all to Shelley's liking, who had envisaged metaphysical discussion but instead had his nerves shaken to pieces as the group regaled themselves with vats of claret until three in the morning. 'I have lived too long near Byron' Shelley wrote as he decided to extricate himself from Byron's 'detested intimacy' and moved to Lerici on the Bay of La Spezia.

Women were excluded from these soirées and Teresa in her little house on the Arno had to rely on the friendship of Jane Williams, whom she found 'sweet', and Mary Shelley, whom she found 'prim'. Mary Shelley however was not immune to Byron's magnetism, admitting that he had the powers to arouse deep and shifting emotions in her, but his ruthless behaviour towards Claire Clairmont and the subsequent abandonment of Allegra had stirred her soul to anger.

TWENTY-TWO

In his journal Byron had written that if he 'erred' it should be heart which would herald the way. The greatest blemish of that complex and tormenting heart was towards his Allegra, whom, though he called her his 'natural daughter', he treated with contemptible cruelty. She was the pawn by which to punish the 'odd-headed' and later, 'damned bitch' Clairmont who had come prancing after him and got herself pregnant.

Allegra was a precocious little girl, given to vanity and love of distinction, traits he could surely ascribe to himself. In her *Vie*, Teresa Guiccioli would claim that Allegra reminded him too much of her mother and that he left the room in disgust whenever she came in. He had her sent from Venice to Ravenna and when he went to live in the Palazzo Guiccioli for a time Teresa made a show of loving her, taking her for drives in her carriage on the Corso, each afternoon. Allegra was a great favourite with everyone on account of the fairness of her skin, which shone, as Byron wrote, 'among the dusky children like the milky way'. But she was also prone to fevers, which worried Claire exceedingly, blaming the climate of Ravenna which was as 'objectionable' as that of Venice. Byron told everyone that he would not tolerate such objections from that source, yet in the end it was Allegra herself who precipitated her own banishment. She was, as he told Hoppner, 'perverse to a degree' and with Teresa's help he secured a place for her in the Capuchin convent at Bagnacavallo, twelve miles from Ravenna. It was Pellegrino Ghigi who brought the four-and-a-half-year-old child, in her nice dress and coral necklace, with her dolls.

In a letter to Shelley, Byron said it was a temporary move and to Hoppner and all others there were the usual platitudes about inculcating learning, morals and religion in her. Shelley was her one visitor, bringing her a gift of a gold chain and finding her not so precocious as before, but 'shy and serious'. She expressed the wish that her Papa and Mammina, meaning Teresa, would pay her a visit, while her real Mammina was writing Byron letters that veered from the imploring to the outraged. Byron was intransigent, vowing that Allegra would never quit his custody and Claire, becoming more desperate, thought up madcap schemes such as having Allegra kidnapped or forging a letter in Byron's handwriting, saying he wished her to be sent home. After he left Ravenna for Pisa, Shelley asked him to place the child in a convent at Lucca, but Byron refused the request, because Allegra out of sight, could also be out of mind.

In February 1822, Claire wrote a letter that was heartbreaking and weirdly prophetic – 'I assure you I can no longer resist the internal inexplicable feeling which haunts me that I shall never see her anymore. I entreat you to destroy this feeling by allowing me to see her.' Byron did not respond, merely saying that Claire could not live without making a scene. Shelley, in an uncustomary outburst, said he would with pleasure knock Byron down and Mary saw that Byron was remorseless and unprincipled.

In a strange twist of fate Claire had travelled secretly to

Pisa, to join the Shelleys on the Bay of Spezia for the summer, when Byron received the first news from Ghigi that Allegra had been 'ill, dangerously ill'. Byron sent a courier, requesting the nuns to send for Professor Tommasini of Bologna, but presently an express messenger arrived to say that the child had died 'of a convulsive catarrhal attack'. It was Teresa who broke the news to him and in her *Vie* she wrote: 'A mortal paleness spread over his face, his strength failed him and he sunk into a seat ... He remained immovable in the same attitude for an hour and no consolation seemed to reach his ears, far less his heart.'

To Shelley, Byron wrote that the blow was 'stunning and unexpected' but defended himself, brooking no reproach whatsoever in his conduct, his feeling or his intentions towards the child. The Shelleys alone with Captain and Jane Williams were debating how to tell Claire, except that she guessed it by their expressions, yielded to a hysteria and yet soon after, as Mary said, was 'tranquil, more tranquil' than she had ever been.

'The body is embarked – in what ship – I know not – neither could I enter into details' Byron wrote, adding that Teresa had to give instructions to Henry Dunn, a merchant at Leghorn, with regard to conveying the remains to England. Meanwhile he bombarded Murray with instructions – the hearse was to be conveyed from London Wharf to Harrow with no expense spared, a fine hearse and mourning coach, the horses decked with feathers and velvet coverings, wands for the pages and proper mourning garments for the clerk, sexton and beadle at Harrow Church. She was to be buried in a spot in the churchyard on the brow of a hill facing Windsor, where he had spent many boyhood hours. The funeral was to be as private as was consistent with decency.

Yet in contrast to such elaborate arrangements he was having arguments with both the embalmers and the apothecary at Leghorn, claiming he was being overcharged on account of his rank, offering one-third of the fee they proposed, since the remains were those of a child and not an adult. When Ghigi's brother-in-law, a priest, along with another emissary, came to Pisa to meet with Byron, they were turned away by Lega Zambelli, and in a greater breach of feeling, Zambelli asked if good truffles could be procured in the Romagna for his Lordship.

Byron had also composed a eulogy for Allegra to be carved on a marble tablet and placed inside the church door, paraphrasing a verse from Samuel – 'I shall go to her but she shall not return to me.' The Rector, the Revd John William Cunningham, along with the churchwardens did not welcome such impertinence and Murray was told that the inscription Byron proposed would 'be felt by every man of refined taste to say nothing of sound morals to be an offence against time and propriety'. Eventually Allegra was buried inside the church door but without a tablet bearing her name. She was, after all, 'a bastard child'.

In the convent, nuns and pupils were in paroxysms of grief, a statue was made in Allegra's honour, dressed in her clothes, with a white fur tippet and the gold chain that Shelley had given her. Byron was sent the remainder of her clothing, three coloured cotton frocks, a velvet frock, a muslin frock, a cap and gloves, a string of corals, a silver spoon and fork, along with her bed linen and furniture, while Claire had to be content with a likeness of Allegra which the Shelleys had to wrest from him, along with a lock of the child's hair.

A few months later, on her way to Vienna to work as a governess, Claire wrote to a friend saying that though she had tried to admire the scenery, she kept seeing in her mind 'her lost darling'.

A few months later, in July 1822, Trelawny came to tell Byron that Shelley, Captain Williams and a boat boy were missing at sea. Trelawny claimed that Byron's lips quivered and his voice wavered upon hearing the news. The friendship with Shelley had turned sour not only because of Allegra and Claire but because of Shelley's inadequacy in Byron's company, Byron making no secret of the fact that he wished to be the greatest living poet and therefore eclipsing Shelley. Shelley's anger and jealousy would have been magnified had he known that in a letter to Tom Moore Byron had nicknamed him 'Serpeant – a siren voice of forbidden truth'.

The 'siren voice' was no more.

Their friendship may have ruptured but they had once been 'brothers' in their poetic aspirations, both disciples of Rousseau whose doctrines however did not impinge on their private and wayward mores. In their 'Frankenstein summer' of 1816 in Geneva when they met, the friendship was forged, they were kindred spirits and outcasts in pusillanimous English society. The two of them sailed each day in Lake Leman, debating God and free will and fatalism and destiny. Then in the evenings, to amuse themselves in that 'curst, selfish, swinish country of brutes' Byron decided that they should compose ghost stories and read them aloud. It was in Villa Diodati, on the lake shore, near Cologny. The group included Shelley, Mary, the persistent Claire and Polly Dolly, physician and embryo author. In that intoxicating environment Mary would conceive the idea of Frankenstein which was published two years later and which Byron extolled to Murray – 'Me thinks it is a wonderful book and remarkable for a seventeen year old girl.'

Shelley may have noted that Byron was 'mad as the wind' but timber-headed Fletcher, Byron's valet, decided that it was Mr Shelley himself who was loopy, succumbing as he did to hallucination in one of their séances, believing that Mary's nipples were about to be metamorphosed into a pair of eyes. Fletcher had to douche him with water and then administer ether. From a ghoulish sketch of Byron's Polly Dolly stole the idea for his 'Vampyre' which he published in pamphlet form, three years later in England, making it seem it had been written by Byron.

Now Shelley was missing, along with Edward Williams and the boat boy, Charles Vivian, somewhere off the coast of Lerici. Captain Daniel Roberts, the retired naval officer who had built the boat, had warned Shelley not to set out, pointing to the black rags of clouds hanging from the heavens, which always presaged a storm. But they were in a hurry to get to La Spezia, their wives were waiting and Shelley, ever proud of his little skiff, believed that it sailed 'like a witch'.

It was an eighteen-foot open craft to which Roberts had to add sails and a false prow so as to compete with Byron's more elegant vessel, the *Bolivar* with its soaring masts, guns and crested cannon. Hardly had they left the shore than a sea fog descended and thunder burst from the skies. Roberts, from a tower at Leghorn, was the last to sight the little boat bobbing on rough seas and soon after it disappeared from sight.

It would be ten days before the bodies were found, fleshless and mutilated, washed up on different parts of the beach, where according to Tuscan quarantine law they had to be buried in the sand and interred in quicklime. Shelley was recognised by the binding of a copy of Keats's *Lamia* in his pocket and Edward Williams by his black silk necktie, tied in sailor fashion.

Trelawny arranged a Hellenic funeral inspired by Aeschylus and for this he had to receive permission to have the two men exhumed and cremated on the shore, though the unfortunate boat boy received no such honours. On a boiling hot day, the sands literally melting from the heat of the furnace, the party had foregathered, Trelawny having brought oak boxes for Shelley's ashes to be deposited and placed in the Protestant cemetery in Rome, next to their infant son William, as Mary had requested. It was a gruesome and public spectacle, mounted dragoons on guard, foot soldiers with spades and mattocks, health officials and well dressed curious spectators watching from their carriages, though not Mary Shelley and not Jane Williams.

Williams was the first to be placed on the pyre and Byron tried to mask his grief with defiance, identifying Williams by his teeth, and looking at the mass of putrid flesh fed piecemeal to the fire, he said it might just as easily have been the carcase of a sheep. Then to rid his body of 'black bile' Byron decided 'to test the power of the waves' and swam a mile or so out, when presently he was sick.

Next day as Shelley was exhumed from the sands, Byron was even more outrageous, asking that he be given Shelley's skull as a souvenir, but it became shattered by the impact of the mattocks. Trelawny, ever theatrical, poured oil, wine and frankincense onto the flames, which made them glisten, then summoning the forces of earth, air and water, he prophesied that Shelley, though changed to a different form, would not be annihilated. In his book *Records of Shelley, Byron and The Author* (published in 1878), he would write of the lonely majestic scenery all about, which harmonised with Shelley's genius, while in the next breath he described the brain, which 'literally seethed, bubbled and boiled'. Shelley's heart although bedded in fire refused to burn and as Trelawny snatched it from thc fiery furnance, Leigh Hunt, with unwonted egotism, claimed it as his.

That evening, the three men, Byron, Hunt and Trelawny, went by carriage to Viareggio where they dined and drank to great excess and according to Hunt 'laughed and shouted, engendering a morbid gaiety' to efface their sorrow.

It was Byron who would accord to Shelley the most beautiful epitaph, describing him in a letter to Tom Moore as 'clear living flame . . . a man about whom the world was ill-naturedly and ignorantly and brutally mistaken'.

TWENTY-THREE

Casa Saluzzo, in the hills of Albaro, overlooking the harbour of Genoa, was to be Byron's last abode in Italy. The journey from Pisa in his ostentatious coach, with his furnishings and menagerie of animals, had the extra whimsicality of three pet geese in a swinging cage hanging from the back. It was late September, roads were flooded, the coach lumbering over mountain passes and past steep precipices, Byron's irritation compounded by their being stopped by customs officials at the various borders. In the towns which they passed, the 'damned Englishers' threw open the windows of their inns to gape at the infamous and saturnine Lord, while he for his part hid in his carriage, because of his morbid dread of them.

The spies appointed by the Vatican seemed to have known more of Byron's moods and movements than he did himself. Torelli, the master spy assigned to him in Pisa, wrote to his colleagues in Genoa to apprise them of his arrival – 'Mylord has at length decided to leave for Genoa. It is said he is already tired of his new favourite the Guiccioli. He has expressed his intention of not remaining long in Genoa but of going to Athens to purchase adoration from the Greeks.'

At Lucca, by arrangement, he met with the Gambas, Count Ruggero, Count Pietro Gamba and Teresa, who had gone on ahead, then a journey by sea to Lerici, where they met with Leigh Hunt and his 'blackguard' family, who had travelled with Trelawny on Byron's boat, the *Bolivar.* In a reckless moment, Byron challenged Trelawny to a swimming competition, a feat which left him sick for four days, confined 'to the worst room in the worst hotel', dosing himself with purgatives and compresses.

Casa Saluzzo had two separate apartments, one for him and one for the Gamba family. He had rented a second house, Villa Negrotti, for the Hunts, which they shared with Mary Shelley, and relationships became somewhat rancid all round, what with Hunt a hypochondriac, his wife confined to her room and seven untamed children running wild on the marble stairs. Hunt still believed himself to be the rightful keeper of Shelley's heart and was refusing to hand it over to Mary. Moreover, he accused her of never having shown Shelley enough love, goading her to repent. Trelawny, a braggart and mischief maker, carried malicious stories and said unfairly that Byron's treatment of his friends was 'shameful'.

The 23-year-old Teresa chafed at being stranded in that unheated villa with stone floors and high ceilings, rain and storm outside, her father and brother despondent at being uprooted from their beloved Romagna and she visiting Byron only by invitation, for a stroll in the lemon gardens. His letters no longer brimmed with tender effusions, instead short bulletins about a head cold, or his swollen eye or the discrepancy between his 'tottle' of the household expenses and that of Lega Zambelli, his bookkeeper, whom he now distrusted.

Byron was at a nadir, believing himself to be 'the most unpopular writer going', yet as he told Douglas Kinnaird, increasingly in love with lucre because one must love something. He needed the lucre as he maintained three families and this in turn made him somewhat miserly and, as he said to Kinnaird, driven to curious fits of accounting and retrenchment of his financial affairs. Hunt complained that the allowance Byron had promised him was coming in 'driblets', Trelawny needed bonds for the upkeep of the *Bolivar* and Mary Shelley, grief-stricken and shattered by the loss of her husband, had turned against Byron, unfairly accusing him of 'unconquerable avarice'.

Trelawny described him as 'peevish, sickly and indifferent' and it is true that he kept more and more to himself. He ate alone and sparingly, worked through the night on *Don Juan*, ten cantos of which were now completed, fuelling his brain with gin and water. He had grown churlish with his English friends, tried to have loans repaid, including the thousand pounds from the ludicrous Wedderburn Webster, whose languid wife Frances had long since left him, her beguilements rumoured to be the reason why Wellington arrived late on the field of Waterloo. With his publisher John Murray he quarrelled increasingly, threatening at times to withdraw; Murray understandably aggrieved, pointed out that it was impossible for Byron to have a more attached friend, unwisely adding that their 'fame and [their] names [were] interlinked'. His hope that Byron might write a 'Volume of manners' of his adopted country was met with scorn.

Conviviality came in the person of Lady Blessington, an 'Irish Asphasia' who contrived to meet him when she came to Genoa with her ménage a trois, a husband, Count Blessington, something of a tippler and the young French 'Cupidon déchainé' Count D'Orsay, whom husband and wife referred to, dotingly, as 'Our Alfred'. Lady Blessington has been vilified as a social climber, one who lied about her lineage and as a writer had a mere 'gossip-columnist skills'. She saw that Byron was flippant, easily put into bad humour but that also he was a lonely man. She was the first woman to write about him and to depict him in unheroic guise, his clothes hanging off him, his hair going grey, a broken dandy, with his outdated Regency slang. In her book *Conversations with Lord Byron* published in 1833, she said her intention was 'to palliate rather than darken his errors'. It was she who got from him his most candid and perspicacious opinion of women. She and he rode together in the Lomellini Gardens where she noted that he was not nearly so accomplished a horseman as he had pretended. She sensed as well, his unquenchable thirst for celebrity, which he was not always nice in procuring. She dined with him in the evening and soon won his confidence so artlessly that she incurred the wrath of Teresa, who refused to be introduced to the 'Blessington Circus'. He was four years into his 'foreign liaison' and as he said, 'Exceedingly governed and kept tight in hand.'

Even at the very zenith of his passion he was ambiguous about it, on the one hand telling Hobhouse in a letter from Ravenna, in 1819, that to leave Teresa or be left by her would drive him quite out of his senses, yet at the same time smarting at his cicisbean existence, saying that a man 'should not consume his life at the side and on the bosom of a woman'.

For Byron Lady Blessington's visit was a little renaissance, as he warmed at hearing the latest London gossip, her salon a rival to Lady Holland's, stories of amours and treacheries, a nostalgia for his heydays, as he recalled this or that gathering, Madame de Staël talking folios, asking the valet de chambre at Lady Davy's to pull out the protruding basque of her corset, much to the disdain of other ladies.

Lady Blessington was the daughter of an impecunious

wastrel in County Tipperary, who had sold her off to a Captain Farmer to pay his gambling debts. She soon escaped, bettered herself, changed her name from Margaret to Marguerite and infiltrated the London circles where she earned the appellation of 'gorgeous', capturing Lord Blessington, from whom there were seemingly no great conjugal demands. Being a snob, she felt compelled to draw comparisons between her bed and Byron's, which his Genoese banker, a Mr Barry, had allowed her to glimpse. Her silvered bed, she tells us, rested on the backs of large swans, every feather in alto-relievo, chastely beautiful, whereas Byron's bed was the most gaudily vulgar thing, emblazoned with his family motto and canopied with a hotchpotch of fussy draperies.

But as he did with everyone when he chose, Byron bewitched her. On their rides she describes his voice, high and effeminate, his musical laughter, his wit, his indiscretions, his eagerness for gossip and the small ribbings that he could never resist, saying that Tom Moore's verses were so very sweet because his father, a Dublin grocer, had fed him sugar plums as a child, and Hobhouse, now a Member of Parliament, had become tedious from listening to parliamentary mummeries. But she was not without insight and saw a man in whom ebullience, sarcasm and melancholy were inextricably wedded. She noted his rages, which when they struck were ungovernable, yet his believing himself to be a victim of persecution wherever he went, insisting that there was a confederacy out to get him and then next day asking her with childlike contrition if she thought he was mad.

To her also Byron opened his mind about love, 'the never dying worm that eats the heart'. Worn out with feelings, he admitted that his disposition and his habits were not those requisite to form the happiness of a woman. He needed *la chasse*, but he also needed solitude and as for many another poet before or since, the first throes of love were the most sublime. Sixteen years after he had lost Mary Chaworth to Mr Musters, and exiled from England, Byron wrote with an aching poignancy of that parting –

> I saw two beings in the hues of youth
> Standing upon a hill, a gentle hill,
> Green and of mild declivity.

He did not discuss every woman with Lady Blessington, but only those with whom he had been emotionally involved. Believing himself to have been a martyr to 'absurd womankind', he gave voice to contradictory, adoring and searing sentiments. Byron besotted was one thing, but Byron thwarted was quite another.

Upon seeing his cousin, Lady Anne Wilmot, at Lady Sitwell's gathering in London in 1813, he was struck by her appearance in mourning, her black dress shot with dewy spangles, and though he had not spoken a word to her, went to his rooms in Albany, and that night fortified with brandy he began his most beautiful and crystalline lyric – 'She walks in beauty, like the night.'

Byron's evaluation of women tended to be severe. They hated anything stripped of its tinsel of sentiment, their bursting albeit fickle hearts desponding over their idols, but not for long. The reading or non-reading of a book, he said, never kept a single petticoat down. True, they kissed better than men, but that was because of an innate worship of images. Moreover, he looked on love as a hostile transaction because of the necessary spice of jealousy. Angels and fiends, he could not trust women, any more than he could trust himself.

Sentiment, he believed, constituted women's entire empire because they failed to understand the comedy of passion. He scoffed at blue-stockings, and chancing on a treatise on the state of women in ancient Greece, who were only permitted books of piety and cookery, allowing for a little gardening, he jovially added, 'why not some road mending, ploughing, hay making and milking?' He was romantic and avowedly anti-romantic, but in the one half of his eroticised psyche, women were essential to him and apart from his time at Harrow he was never without their favours and their persecutions. Even in the Levant, along with youths and rouged jugglers, he took mistresses, landladies or their daughters, prostitutes or the disaffected wives of aristocrats.

His sexual initiation was a compound of the pure and the prurient. The mooning love for cousins contrasted starkly with his nurse May Gray's secretive and lewd advances, something he reluctantly confided to his lawyer Hanson, describing how she came to his bed to 'play tricks with [his] person'. In daytime she fed him dire Calvinist sermons, providing an uncomprehending brew of guilt and desire, alternating with scenes of jealousy as she brought home drunken coach boys from Nottingham to carouse with.

Before he was twenty-one he fathered a son by Lucinda, a maid at Newstead Abbey, to whom he gave an annuity of £100 to save her from the workhouse. In a poem, the child, a son, was hailed as 'Fair cherub, Child of love', but he never referred to it again. His next relationship was also with one of his Newstead servants, the 'ornamental' Susan Vaughan, 'a witch and intriguer' who betrayed him with a younger and more vigorous man. His verses were then laden with reproach and self-pity, his wounds like no others, and writing to his friend Francis Hodgson he said never to mention a woman to him again or to allude to the existence of that sex.

From every woman he derived something that would fuel his embattled and ambiguous feelings. From Mary Ann Chaworth he bore the bitter brunt of humiliation, having overheard her dismiss him as 'that lame boy', from Caroline Lamb he had his fill of demented possessiveness, from Augusta, love and then as he saw it, abnegation of love, and from Annabella Milbanke, with her ongoing construct of righteousness, a woman's unforgivingness. Even when his blood was 'all meridian' with regard to Teresa, he was somewhat disparaging about her in a letter to Augusta. Despite Teresa's manifest adoration, he guessed that without him she would fasten her affections on another, which indeed she did, 'philandering lightly' with other Englishmen, including Henry Fox, Lord Holland's son, and later the Earl of Malmesbury. When she was enamoured with the French poet Lamartine, she helped him on his sequel to *Childe Harold*, which he called *Le Dernier Chant du pèlerinage d'Harold*, and at the age of forty-seven she married the forty-nine-year-old Marquis de Boissy and lived opulently. According to her stepson Ignazio Guiccioli, her face was so enamelled that it impaired her smile, as she was driven around Paris in a green carriage lined with white satin, modelled on Lady Blessington's carriage. Having elevated herself and Byron to the spheres of Petrarch and Laura or Dante and Beatrice, she would in time commune with him at séances, so as to enable her to write her own account of their life together. In the *Vie de Lord Byron*, published in Paris in 1868, the dissimulating Teresa, as Iris Origo tells it in *The Last Attachment*, painted a picture of a relationship with Byron that was 'romantic and idealised'. To the end, surrounded with her various relics, letters, pressed flowers and a full-length portrait of Byron, she persisted in the fiction of their love being pure and unstained.

But in 1823 Lady Blessington, by not being his lover and by not wishing to be, was the one who noted his parched spirits and his heart running to waste for want of being allowed to extend itself. It was to her he first confided his plan to go to Greece as an emissary of the Greek Committee in London and unnervingly, he dreamt that he would die in Greece.

TWENTY-FOUR

In high-hearted youth Byron had dreamt of being Greece's saviour and this fervour was re-ignited in 1821 at the commencement of the Greek War of Independence. The Greek insurrection, which had begun two years earlier, had however been beset by failure, but the Greeks still strove for independence from the Ottoman Empire and their plight caught the imagination of intellectuals and liberals throughout Europe. Officers from Napoleon's scattered armies, idealists and mystics had gone there to join the various tribal chieftains in their ongoing insurgency, Greece occupying part of western Greece and the Turks still holding the eastern part of the country. Byron's ongoing interest and concern were relayed to Hobhouse in letters, who in turn told the Greek Committee in London, since they were anxious to enlist Byron as their emissary and ally in that 'theatre of war'.

The correspondent, Captain Edward Blaquiere, who had been canvassing support in Europe, was asked to visit Byron in Genoa and there he outlined the situation of a desperate and beleaguered Greece, her erstwhile sporadic victories as nothing if foreign aid, arms, armoured sea boats and foreign officers did not come to her assistance. 'Command me' Byron wrote at once to the Greek Committee, saying he would not merely give his name or his money to the cause, he would go to the Levant in person. This was the elixir. It signalled escape from the demands and tedium of everyday life and was a metamorphosing from poet to soldier. Blaquiere followed with a letter – saying that Byron's presence would 'operate as a talisman in that field of glory'. Intoxicating words and for Byron the fervour of his revolutionary youth was restored, except of course that he foresaw 'objections of a domestic nature'.

What neither Byron nor the Greek Committee in London foresaw were delays, bewildering and contradictory strategies, tribal leaders who were either weak and irresolute or ruthless, rival factions and armies of untrained youths who wanted belts, blades and rations. 'Speculators and percolators', Byron would call them, leaders with a considerable shyness with the truth, so that a No could be modified to a Yes in a moment and vice versa.

Four Greek leaders, though ostensibly united, had their own agendas – Colocotronis in the Morea; Botsaris, a Suliote; bandit Odysseus, primate of Athens; and Prince Alexander Mavrocordatos, who had given Greek lessons to Mary Shelley and was now bombarding Byron with unctuous and flattering letters.

There in Genoa, his mind agog, Byron commenced on his plans, using his own money to ensure medical stores and gunpowder for a thousand men for two years, chartering a boat from a shipping merchant in Leghorn, arranging with Mr Barry, his Genoese banker, for bills of dollars to the sum of fifty thousand, along with Spanish gold coins. He engaged a fledgling physician, Dr Bruno, who would be in perpetual terror of Byron and his three dogs. In a bow to splendour, he ordered scarlet uniforms with buttons, epaulettes and sashes and fearsome helmets with waving plumes, for his corps of three, Count Gamba, Edward Trelawny and himself. The helmets were modelled on those in Book VI of the *Iliad*, which had so frightened the infant Astyanax, and even the flashy Trelawny baulked at them and so they were put back in the pink cardboard box, never to be introduced to Greek climes.

As the covert plans progressed, the question was how to tell Teresa. She would swoon, she would cry, she would succumb to fits, she would beg him not to go, or if he must, to take her with him. She swooned, she cried, she clung and eventually numb with grief she lay on a sofa, until she was escorted in hysterics by her father to a waiting carriage, bound for Ravenna.

He had enlisted the ever-credulous Count Gamba, who was still smarting from the failure of the Romagna insurrection, and Trelawny, who appeared to share his enthusiasm, but was in fact writing to Claire Clairmont, to whom he had bizarrely proposed marriage, saying that once in Greece, he would shift for himself, which indeed he did, joining bandit Odysseus. There was also Trelawny's black groom Benjamin, Fletcher, who predicted that they were going to a country of 'rockets and robbers', Lega Zambelli, Byron's bookkeeper, Tita the former gondolier who thought Mylord 'amiably mad', Dr Bruno and Prince Schilizzi, a relative of Mavrocordatos, an ardent monarchist, who flattered Byron by telling him that the Greeks would crown him King.

The vessel *Hercules* was 'a tub of a ship', shaped like a baby's cradle. Though superstitious about setting out on a journey on Friday the thirteenth, the party boarded at Genoa early that morning. With blazing sunshine and no breeze, the water glassy and unruffled, they were stalled until evening, when however a storm arose, the winds so forceful that the boat was tossed from side to side and the horses thrown into such a frenzy that they kicked at their partitions. Passengers had to disembark as carpenters were found to repair the horse boxes, and Byron in elegiac mood, walked in the Lomellini Gardens, where he had ridden with Lady Blessington, then wandered through the empty salons of Villa Saluzzo, with its traces of Teresa, including a lock of her hair, which he did not take with him. The era for romantic keepsakes was over.

Three days later, on 16 July 1823, they set out. Byron, the 'Pilgrim', as Trelawny called him, in deference to Shelley's 'Pilgrim of Eternity', was in a black mood, lifted only when they touched down at Leghorn and he received a laudatory verse that Goethe, his 'liege lord', had written for him, though no one was at hand to translate it from the German. Nevertheless, Byron withdrew to his cabin to write in homage to the 'Illustrious Sir' of Weimar, apologising for the hasty prose, surrounded by hurry and bustle, going, as he said, to Greece and hoping to be of some little use to that 'struggling country'.

The empty days were filled with small diversions, he boxed with Trelawny, fenced with Gamba, fired his pistols at the gulls, bathed when the waters were calm, in daytime kept to his abstemious diet of cheese, cucumber and cider, took some grog in the evening. Passing Stromboli and the smoking summit of Etna, he remained on deck all night, absorbing colour and atmosphere for a last canto of *Don Juan*, though poetry was soon to be abandoned. To Trelawny he admitted that if death were to come in Greece in the shape of a cannonball, then death was welcome, asking that his ashes be scattered off the rocky island of Maina in the southern

Peloponnese, Trelawny maintaining that they would be claimed by Westminster Abbey.

On 3 August they arrived at Argostoli, the chief port of Cephalonia, with its whitewashed houses set against arid brown mountains, and seeing the Morea in the distance Byron felt elated, believing 'that eleven long years of bitterness' were lifted from his shoulders. Captain Pitt Kennedy, secretary to the English Resident Colonel Napier, came aboard the ship to welcome Byron and his group. Colonel Napier, he said, was ready to serve them in any way, while having to appear to show neutrality, since the Ionian Islands, under British protectorate, were neutral and could not be seen to be partisan with the Greeks. The news however was not encouraging, the Greeks were war-shy, hiding in the hills, the Turks had regained the coast and had undisputed command of the seas. Greek leaders, far from uniting with one another, were engaged in a vicious cycle of backstabbing, their one common agenda being the pressing need for funds. Pending loans from the London Committee, Byron had to advance more money towards Mavrocordatos, to equip a naval squadron to attack the Turks. He reckoned that already he had given more to the Greek cause than that with which Bonaparte had begun his Italian campaign. The interim in Cephalonia, supposed to have been a matter of weeks, dragged on for five months, Byron writing to the Greek Committee in London to explain away the delays, masking his frustration by saying that it was 'better playing at nations than gaming at Almack's'. There were indeed beautiful and glistening moonlights, azure waters, azure skies; small Greek triumphs, Prince Alexander Mavrocordatos had ventured into high seas and taken a Turkish ship with its twelve guns, but as Byron said this was 'not quite Thermopylae'.

He decided on an expedition to Ithaca. It entailed a nine-hour journey in scorching heat, on mules, across the island to San Eufemia and then by boat over the straits to Ithaca. Treated to figs and wine, singing like a Homeric armada, they arrived on the fabled island with their trestle beds, their trunks and Byron's more elaborate bed, since it was decided that they would sleep in caves and decline the hospitality of the English Governor. It was not the Homeric ruins or the grottoes of the nymphs, or the 'twaddle' spouted by English antiquarians that struck Byron, it was the appalling wreckage and devastation of war. The island was swarming with Greek refugees, destitute and without a roof over their heads, throwing themselves at his mercy, their plaints so extreme, so pitiful, that he deposited money with Mr Knox, the Resident, to be distributed for their relief. He rescued the Chalandritsanos family, a widow with three daughters, had them sent to Cephalonia and maintained at his expense. It was the fifteen-year-old Loukas, the widow's son, then training in the mountains to be a warrior, who would eventually seek out Byron and become the object of 'love, fathomless love', which was how Byron had described that particular malady in Venice in 1816.

On their return journey at the Monastery of Theotokos Aqvilion near Sami, Byron suffered the first of the convulsive fits that would be a precursor of even worse seizures. They had been welcomed by wafts of incense, then an elaborate ceremony, with hymns of glorification, the Abbot proclaiming the '*Lordo Inglese*', when Byron flew into a rage, shouting to be released from this 'pestilential madman' as he stormed to a nearby room. There he barricaded himself in, stacking chairs and a table against the door. He refused to allow Dr Bruno to enter and give him his pills, then tore his clothes, tore the mattress that was on the floor, stood half naked in a corner, like a hunted animal, calling them 'fiends', saying he was 'in hell'. Hamilton Brown, a young Scotsman and soldier who had joined the *Hercules* at Leghorn, eventually restrained him, gave him Dr Bruno's '*benedette pillule*' and after uttering some childish drivel, Byron lay down and fell asleep on the mattress, Hamilton Brown's reward was to be let sleep on Byron's portmanteau bed.

Back in Cephalonia, he awaited news from the fragile and rivalrous Greek coalition. The Greek Committee in London somewhat disapproving, asking why he lingered so long on the island, some suspecting him of merely having gone there to bask in the Ionian Islands and accrue material for his poetry. 'For all this I do not despair' he wrote in his journal, except that he did despair, the revolutionary zeal was gone, the platoons of foreign soldiers had dwindled, some killed by Turks, some by Greeks, some by disease and some by suicide.

According to Mavrocordatos, the point in the fatherland most weak and most threatened by the enemy was Missolonghi, on the Gulf of Patras, to which he was asking Byron to come as its saviour and secure the destiny of Greece. So after five months, on 29 December, they set out, their two boats bearing the neutral Ionian flag, Byron and his party in one and Count Gamba with all their provisions and thousands of dollars in the second boat. The journey was dogged with hazards. There were fleas, there were floods, there were storms and then the pursuit by enemy frigates, Byron and his group escaping to shallower waters and scampering onto the Scorfa rocks, where Byron dispatched an urgent message to Colonel Stanhope on Missolonghi, who had been sent from England to be his fellow commander there. Byron asked that they be safely escorted, expressing his greatest concern for Loukas, saying 'I would rather see him cut in pieces and myself too than have him taken out by barbarians', words that with their romantic inference can hardly have pleased the doctrinaire Stanhope, who had come to save and enlighten the Greeks. Gamba's boat was captured, the captain brought onto the Turkish frigate to be interrogated before being beheaded, the catastrophe averted only because that captain had once rescued the Turkish captain on the Black Sea. Instead of their boat, with Gamba, Lega Zambelli, the contingent of servants, horses, guns, money, printing press, cannons, arms and Byron's secret correspondence with the Greeks being confiscated, they were treated to dinner and a pipe, then with oriental ceremony, allowed on their way. Byron, not normally religious, put it down to the good offices of St Dionysus and the Madonna of the Rocks.

The initial welcome was indeed heartening, Byron in his scarlet regimental uniform, escorted by canoe to Missolonghi, arriving to the salute of guns, a rejoicing crowd, Mavrocordatos, Colonel Stanhope and a long line of Greek and foreign officers to conduct him to the humble two-storey house above damp ground, with stables for the horses and a courtyard for the drilling of an army. Trelawny, who would come later, described it as 'the worst spot on the surface of the earth', a dismal swamp surrounded by stagnant pools, looking out on a slime cold sea, and calling it 'the belt of death'. Mavrocordatos, though full of flourishes and flattery, struck Byron, with his shy eyes and tiny round spectacles, as being more scholar than soldier. Soon he was visited by primates and chiefs with their suite of soldiers, all scrounging for money, and though he had vowed not to join a faction but to join a nation, he now found himself a partisan of Mavrocordatos. His first task was to form an artillery corps that he would lead and train for the proposed siege and eventual capture of Lepanto, a name that resonated throughout history. In 1571 Don Juan of Austria led a European fleet that had defeated the Ottomans, and Donny Johnny Byron was expected to repeat that heroic feat. Lepanto was a fortified town twenty-five miles east of Missolonghi, the fortress now in Turkish hands was garrisoned by Albanian troops, who were rumoured to be unhappy with their wretched circumstances.

The army, enrolled under his personal banner, were Suliote tribesmen, exiled from the cliffs of southern Albania, who had taken refuge in Cephalonia and whose picturesque costumes and renown for courage appealed to the romantic in him. Unfortunately, he had based his estimation of all Suliotes on two whom he had taken into service on his travels in 1809, and the army that he now found himself leader of and had to personally provide for were undisciplined, cynical and grasping. They cared nothing for Greek independence, pressed him constantly for higher wages and better rations, were obsessed with tribal status and mutinied at being under the governance of German, English, American, Swiss and Swedish officers. Along with drilling and training, he had to house six hundred soldiers and their horses, their rations alone costing two thousand dollars a week. With the help of an Italian, wife of the local tailor, he had to recruit 'unencumbered women' to be at their disposal.

'Revolutions are not to be made with rose water,' he said, Mocked by his army, trapped in a relative barracks, Byron was surrounded by swords, pistols, sabres, dirks, rifles, guns, blunderbusses, helmets and trumpets. He had the double task of maintaining discipline and instilling a martial fervour, to get them to the field. The trumpets could not be sounded until they had taken Lepanto.

An English surgeon, Daniel Forrester, who came ashore briefly with his captain on the gun brig *Alacrity*, gives a vivid description of that rather haphazard ménage, young soldiers in white fustanellas and dirty socks, armed to the teeth, either banging their muskets or sitting on the floor playing cards. Tita, in full livery, ushered Forrester and Captain Yorke in, Loukas, dressed as an Albanian, handsomely chased arms in his girdle, served them coffee and olives, Byron receiving them cordially but talking in such a 'harem scarem' manner that it was hard to believe he had ever written anything on a 'grave or affecting subject'. After dinner, the amusement was to fire at maraschino bottles and Byron's aim was surprisingly exact, but as Forrester noted, his hand shook 'as if under the influence of an ague fit'.

According to information from Greek spies, the capture of Lepanto would not prove difficult, as the Albanian army which manned it had not been paid for months and were close to starvation. They would, it was said, merely put up a token fight, and be happy to surrender. Lepanto taken, they could, according to Mavrocordatos, seize Patras and the castle of the Morea, whence western Greece would be in their hands. The picture of Byron in that fetid lagoon, rain pouring down, the streets like mire, an army bent on discord and disunion, would seem, were it not so lamentably true, like a tale imagined by the young excitable Lord Byron when he rode his pony in the countryside around Aberdeen.

Many things conspired to dishearten him, but worst of all was the violent agitation of feeling for Loukas, Byron believing that as with Edleston and Robert Rushton, his wonted magnetism would captivate the young page, except that it hadn't. For Loukas, Byron was an old man, his hair greying, his teeth discoloured, a tendency to corpulence, merely a potentate to supply uniforms, gold helmets and all the trappings for a warrior. To Byron Loukas's frown was as disquieting 'as an adder's eye'. On his thirty-sixth birthday in January 1824, though mindful of his waning sexual powers, he wrote a poem on the persistence of love, even in a heart grown old:

> 'Tis time this heart should be unmoved,
> Since others it hath ceased to move;
> Yet, though I cannot be beloved,
> Still let me love!
>
> . . .
>
> The fire that on my bosom preys
> Is lone as some volcanic isle;
> No torch is kindled at its blaze –
> A funeral pile.

Honour, obstinacy, a certain fondness for the rascally Greeks and a responsibility towards the Committee in London kept him there, vowing 'I mean to stick by the Greeks to the last rag and the last shirt'. His spirits were temporarily buoyed, when after a delay of six months there came news of the arrival of the great fire-master Mr Parry and his team of mechanics. Mr Parry was to bring every species of destructive arms, spoilt powders that would be made serviceable in a 'laboratory', which he would oversee, along with the manufacture of Congreve rockets. Unfortunately, Parry had never been near a Congreve rocket, he had merely been a clerk in the Woolwich civil department and neither he, Byron nor the Greek Committee had thought of providing coal to fuel an arsenal. Parry quarrelled with the entire household, but much to the irritation of Colonel Stanhope, Byron befriended him, both of them drinking brandy through the night and Parry, 'a rough burly fellow', regaling Byron with his fund of 'pothouse stories' and gossip from England.

On 13 February, an advance guard led by Count Gamba was ordered to set out for Lepanto, Byron and his troops primed to follow the next day. But treachery had struck. Colocotronis, learning of it, concluded that if Lepanto were captured it would put his rival Mavrocordatos in the ascendancy and his own authority over western Greece would be sabotaged. He sent a small party of Suliotes from the Peloponnese over to Missolonghi to spread unrest among Byron's Suliote army and to dissuade them from fighting. At the hour of departure they rebelled, said they would not march unless they received higher pay, then demanded that several men from each rank be promoted to general, colonel or captain, ensuring exorbitant wages. But even if those terms were met, they were not prepared to fight against stone walls, to risk their lives to secure Lepanto's crumbling Venetian fortress, which was devoid of booty. Byron, feeling betrayed by this bunch of swindlers, washed his hands of them and only after immense persuasion from one of their chieftains did he agree to form a new corps, but with a lesser body of men. The plan was postponed, but the momentum was gone.

The 'volcanic mind of Lord Byron', as Gamba said, was thrown into a state of commotion and the following night Gamba found him lying on a divan in his ill-lit room, crushed and broken by both public and private failure. Later on he rose, drank some brandy and cider, when Parry noticed a change in his countenance and when he stood up he collapsed, foamed at the mouth and thrashed around the floor so violently that Parry and Tita had to hold him down, while Dr

Bruno and a Dr Millingen, who had been added to his corps, debated the niceties of the fit, unable to agree on whether it was apoplexy or epilepsy. As he lay there, a messenger rushed to the room to say the Suliotes had gone into the town to seize all the arms and ammunition stored in the depot; and they all ran out in consternation, leaving Byron alone. Presently, two drunken German soldiers, who had touted the false alarm about the seizure of the depot, burst into his room, waving and shouting and in what must have seemed a waking hallucination, they told him that he was now under their jurisdiction.

There followed then a series of what he called 'strange weathers and strange incidents'. A small civil war erupted in the town of Missolonghi between civilians and Byron's soldiers when a Suliote soldier taking a small boy to see the arsenal fell into an argument with a Swiss officer, drew his yatagan, severing the Swiss's arm, and then shooting him in the head. He was summarily arrested, but his compatriots hearing of it assembled and threatened to burn the building unless he was at once released. Parry's mechanics, though not Parry himself, had scooted, not being accustomed to that 'kind of slashing', and a few days later there was an earthquake, to which soldiers and citizens responded by firing muskets, the way, as Byron said, savages howled at an eclipse of the moon. As the walls quivered, the whole town rocked, men and women reeling as if from wine, Byron, the spurned lover, went around the deserted hall, searching for Loukas, and it was to him that Byron's last poem was addressed, lines as intense and moving as any he had written to Mary Chaworth or Augusta or Teresa. For all his swagger and bravura, Byron's real theme was love:

I watched thee on the breakers, when the rock
Received our prow and all was storm and fear,
And bade thee cling to me through every shock;
This arm would be thy bark, or breast thy bier.

. . .

Thus much and more; and yet thou lov'st me not,
And never wilt! Love dwells not in our will.
Nor can I blame thee, though it be my lot
To strongly, wrongly, vainly love thee still.

There remained one last treason in this theatre of war. A Greek chieftain, Georgios Karaiskakis, combined forces with a renegade Suliote leader, Djavella, who in retaliation for some wrong done him by Greek boatmen, decided to lay siege to the town, to paralyse Byron's private army and most importantly to create division between him and Mavrocordatos. They seized hostages, occupied a fort at the entrance to the lagoon, where they were joined by a Turkish fleet, whereupon anarchy ensued in the town, the local people barricading themselves in their houses for fear of being massacred, calling for Byron's protection. As the authorities arrested suspects and seized papers they found, under Byron's very own roof, one Constantine Valpiotti, who confessed that he and Karaiskakis, in treasonable league with the Turks, had embarked on a plot for the joint occupation of Missolonghi, the overthrow of the provisional government, taking Byron as their hostage. It was as if he himself had willed these 'incidents', being as he once described himself 'the careful pilot of my proper woe'.

In order to reassure the panic-stricken citizens and in a

beautiful defiance of the Turkish fleet and what would seem defiance of fate herself, he organised a cavalcade to ride through the town. He rode with his cohorts, which included foot soldiers and cavalry in their white fustanellas, a display of plumes and muskets, Loukas in scarlet livery, Byron himself in a green jacket, fêted by the people who followed beyond the north gates, calling out to him. When within weeks they would be asking for part of the 'honourable cadaver' of their illustrious Lord, to be placed in the local church of San Spiridione.

How guarded his last letter to Teresa – 'The spring is come – I have seen a swallow today – and it was time – for we have had but a wet winter hitherto . . . I do not write to you letters about politics – which would only be tiresome, and yet we have little else to write about – except some private anecdotes which I reserve for "viva voce" when we meet.'

Caught in a downpour as he galloped with Gamba in the olive groves outside Missolonghi, he was soon after seized with cold shuddering fits, for which he was prescribed a hot bath and doses of castor oil. Within days, the fever had worsened and two more doctors were summoned, a Dr Loukas Vaya, who had once been physician to Ali Pasha, and Dr Treiber, surgeon of the artillery brigade, all at variance as to whether he had rheumatic, typhoid or malarial fever. None could agree, except that they bled him frequently, the lancet sometimes going too near the temporal artery, so that the blood could not be stopped, Parry vehemently trying to stop them and Byron in agony crying out 'Close the veins, close the veins'.

A few days later on Easter Sunday the startled and disbelieving group around his bed began to fear the worst or, as Dr Bruno said, the cup of health was passing from His Lordship's lips. Byron himself recalled that long ago a clairvoyant, Mrs Williams, had foretold misfortune for him in his thirty-seventh year. Outside the pestulent sirocco wind was blowing a hurricane, the rain fell with a tropical violence, the bedroom a scene of confusion and despair, Fletcher and Gamba 'unmanned' by grief, Parry and Bruno warring, because Bruno was for abundant bleeding. Byron finally agreed to the fourth bleeding because Bruno warned that if he didn't, the disease might act on his cerebral and nervous system, thereby depriving him of his reason. Thus he lay propped on a pillow, his head bandaged, the leeches along his temples discharging trickles of blood, slipping in and out of delirium, giving confused orders and wishes in both English and Italian, a mêlée of tongues, the baffled onlookers helpless as to what to do.

A deathbed scene that many an artist would have painted, litres of blood in basins, wrung towels, lancets, Byron holding Parry's hand and at times weeping uncontrollably. Delacroix would have done so with a poetic ghastliness, Caravaggio with a forensic cruelty, but only Rembrandt would have caught the fear and bewilderment in the eyes of those onlookers, all of whom venerated Byron but in their zeal and their helplessness differed as to what could or should be done. 'You know my wishes' Byron would say, his commands wild, scattered and contradictory, his mood ranging from the philosophical to the frantic, pressing Parry to get on with building a schooner for their proposed journey to South America, then again believing that the evil eye had been put on him and requesting a witch from Missolonghi be summoned to lift it. He raved and half rose as if he were mounting a breach in an assault, then according to Parry cried out 'My wife, my Ada, my country', while others claimed that he said 'Dear Augusta, poor dear

Ada', then place names, numbers, snatches of Greek and Latin poetry from his Harrow days, a mysterious reference to 'something precious' that he was leaving behind, stuttered syllables, then nothing.

At dusk on Easter Monday, 19 April, amid dark skies and a thunderstorm, Lord Byron, who had been the hope of the Greek nation, who had known 'the idolatry of man and the flattering love of women', breathed his last, passing over, as it was reported, to 'his everlasting tabernacle'. Tita cut off a lock of his hair and removed the cornelian ring, that 'toy of blushing hue', which John Edleston had given him. The golden doubloons and dollars missing from the coffer were thought to have been taken by Loukas, and when questioned by Pietro Gamba, Loukas avowed that Lord Byron had given him that money to assist his starving family. The sad aftermath is that Loukas died in Cephalonia some six months later 'in want of the necessaries of life'.

At Mavrocordatos's orders, the guns were fired over the lagoon at given intervals and answered by volleys of rejoicing cannon from the Turks at Patras and Lepanto. The Greek woman who had laid him out said that the 'corpse was white like the wing of a young chicken' and the citizens of Missolonghi kept asking for his heart. Twenty-one days of mourning were ordered to be held in every church in Greece.

TWENTY-FIVE

'Let not my body be hacked or sent to England – here let my bones moulder', were two injunctions of Byron's that were ignored. Just as the poet Orpheus had his body hacked by women infuriated by the constancy of his love for Eurydice, Byron's body was likewise hacked. His doctors decided on a general autopsy to settle among themselves the bitter dispute as to the cause of his death. They paused, as the young Dr Millingen would write in his *Memoirs of the Affairs of Greece* some seven years later, 'in silent contemplation of this abused clay which still bore witness to the physical beauty which had attracted so many men and women ... the only blemish of his body which might otherwise have vied with that of Apollo himself, was the congenital malformation of his left foot and leg'. In this orgy of lament, Millingen got the foot wrong. The brain and the dura mater was what interested them, thinking, as witch doctors might, to trace the mysteries within the man. They found the cranium could be that of a man of eighty, the heart of great size but flaccid, the liver showing the toll of alcohol, stomach and kidneys impaired. Those honoured organs were placed in urns for embalming, but the lungs allowed to reside in the Church of San Spiridione so that the local citizens might shed their tears over them. No lead coffin being available, the body was placed in a packing case lined with tin, the urns beside it, the lid hermetically closed and fixed with the seals of the Greek authorities.

There was much squabbling as to where Byron should be buried. Trelawny, temporarily forsaking his 'great mission' with Odysseus, travelled for three days, fording torrents and mountain passes, pursued by mad dogs; come supposedly to mourn, but with ghoulish curiosity he asked Fletcher to lift the shroud and allow him to see the deformed foot which Byron had hidden all his life. No marble bust, he claimed, could do justice to the beautiful white face and perfect features. He was of the same opinion as Stanhope that Byron should be buried in the Acropolis; Lord Sydney Osborne, the British Ambassador at Zante, arguing that if the Turks were to recapture Athens, Byron's tomb would be desecrated, Gamba, Parry and Fletcher repeating Byron's conflicting orders; stasis until Lady Byron's wishes were made known.

The coffin, draped with his helmet and the sword with which he had meant to charge on Lepanto, along with a crown of laurels, was placed in San Spiridione. The locals, wishing for his heart to be left there, were given instead his lungs and larynx, which were placed in an urn and stolen not too long afterwards. In churches and in makeshift churches in olive groves, warriors and citizens alike came to hear orations to his greatness, Byron a son of Greece, whose arms would receive him, whose tears would bathe the tomb containing his body and be perpetually shed over his precious heart. Even Stanhope, who was by then in Salona, forgetting their quarrels, waxed eloquent in his letter to the London Committee, saying England had lost her brightest genius, Greece her noblest friend and that what remained were the emanations of a splendid mind.

On 23 May the embalmed remains were brought onto the brig *Florida*, bound for England, the brig, ironically, on which Captain Blaquiere had travelled, bringing with him the first portion of the loan from the Greek Committee.

From Zante, the news had reached Lady Blessington at Naples, Leigh Hunt at Florence, and the Guiccioli family at Ravenna. Mary Shelley's condolence letter and all newspapers were kept away from Teresa until her father was permitted to leave Ferrara so as to tell her himself, except that his courage failed him. The story goes that Teresa had a premonition of it upon seeing an old school friend arrive at her doorstep in the hottest hour of day.

The 'fatal intelligence' came upon England like an earthquake on 14 May, the blue envelope bearing the official letter from Lord Sydney Osborne was delivered to Douglas Kinnaird, who sent it by courier to Hobhouse, who read it in 'an agony of grief'.

There were also letters from Count Gamba and from Fletcher, Gamba saying that Byron had died in a strange land and amongst strangers, but that no man was more loved and more wept over, while Fletcher asked to 'please excuse all defects', followed with a commodious account of Byron's last days.

'Byron is dead. Byron is dead.' Thus did Jane Welsh write to her future husband Thomas Carlyle, who felt as if he had lost a brother, as did Victor Hugo in France, where young men wore black crêpe bands on their hats in mourning. A hasty painting, depicting Byron on his deathbed, was placed in the Passage Feydeau in Paris, where crowds filed past, and in the newspapers it was noted that the two greatest men of the century, Napoleon and Byron, had departed in the same decade. School children were put to reciting verses of *Childe Harold*. Tennyson, aged fifteen, ran into the woods and carved the same grieving sentence on sandstone rock near his father's rectory.

Byron's nephew, Captain George Byron, now the seventh heir, travelled to Kent to tell Annabella, then reported to Hobhouse that he had left her in a 'distressing state' and that she expressed the wish for any account of Byron's final weeks. Sir Francis Burdett broke the news to Augusta at St James's Palace, who clung to a sanctimonious straw, gathered from Fletcher's letter, that Mylord, since his first seizure, had placed the Bible she had given him on the breakfast table each morning. It seems to be the only recorded time that Byron appeared at a breakfast table. Hobhouse advised that she should not disclose such a confidence, convinced as he was that Byron would not make 'superstitious use' of the Holy Book. As a rising young parliamentarian, Hobhouse appointed himself as Byron's keeper.

So in that great flux of grief and condolence, something ugly and incontrovertible was afoot, with Hobhouse as its mastermind, backed, as he wrote triumphantly in his diary, by Murray's decisive conduct. The 'plaguy' Memoirs were for burning.

'After the first excessive grief was over, I determined to lose no time in doing my duty of preserving all that was left to me of my friend – his fame'; so Hobhouse wrote in his diary. At the very same time Sir William Hope, in his esteem for Lady Byron, sent her solicitor, G.B. Wharton, a letter pointing out that it would be most cruel and lamentable for her ladyship to 'undergo any further mortification'. The mortification devolved around Byron's Memoirs, which Mr Murray had told him were written 'in a language so horrid and disgusting' that as a man of honour, he would not publish them.

In 1819 when Tom Moore visited him in his villa at Brenta, near Venice, Byron presented him with 78 folio pages of his Memoirs, written as he said 'in his finest, fiercest, Caravaggio style'. Byron's one stipulation was that they would not be published in his lifetime and he gave Moore the freedom to sell them if he had to. He also gave Moore the discretionary power to change a thing or two, to add what he pleased from his own knowledge of the author and to contradict where necessary. He admitted that a reader would find a host of opinions and some fun in the detailed autopsy of his marriage and its consequences. The summation was no doubt unforgiving but we must remember that Byron did not spare himself either.

Lady Byron had been invited to read 'this long and minute account' of their marriage and separation, with the freedom to detect any falsity and to mark any passages which did not coincide with the truth. The story he wished to tell was for future generations, which neither he nor she could arise from the dust to prove or disprove. She declined to read it, but after conferring with her solicitors thought that such a memoir was wholly unjustifiable and that she would not ever sanction it.

Byron wrote and despatched many more pages to Moore who, finding himself in 'pecuniary difficulties' and with Byron's knowledge, sold them to Murray for two thousand pounds, the agreement being that he could buy them back when he so wished.

In May 1824, while Byron's remains had not even left the port of Zante, the machinations had begun, with Hobhouse and Murray as the masterminds. Augusta had at first dithered, but soon, under the sway of Robert Wilmot-Horton, Byron's avowed enemy, she capitulated. Lady Byron, while professing detachment in the matter, appointed Colonel Doyle to act as her arbiter.

The four men met in Murray's drawing room in Albemarle Street in London along with Moore and the poet Henry Luttrell whom he had brought as an ally to augment his case but who was already wavering. Moore had borrowed two thousand guineas from Longmans the publishers and arrived determined to buy the Memoirs back from Murray, who along with interest was also requesting collateral expenses. Moore was detested by all of Byron's friends and mocked for being the son of a Dublin grocer, hailing, as Leigh Hunt had said, 'from the bogs of Clontarf', a neighbourhood, to my knowledge, free of bogland. Augusta called him that 'detestable little man', yet nevertheless Moore was the one to whom Byron in a letter not long before his death, bequeathed the last 'dregs of affection in [his] heart'.

Moore had interviewed Samuel Rogers, Henry Brougham and Lord Lansdown, all of whom agreed with him that total destruction of the Memoirs was uncalled for. The thrust of his argument was that it was an injustice to condemn the work, to throw it aside as if it were 'a pest bag', and that the burning would throw a stigma on it which it did not deserve. Murray retaliated, saying that Mr Gifford of *The Quarterly Review*, to whom he had sent it, said that it was 'only fit for a brothel'. Moore's various arguments were unavailing as Hobhouse in league with Murray was 'for total suppression of the work'. In the vehement argument that ensued, Moore and Hobhouse almost came to blows as Hobhouse claimed that in September 1822, at their last meeting in Italy, Byron had expressed uneasiness about the gift of the Memoirs and only delicacy for Moore's feelings had kept him from requesting that they be returned.

Wilmot-Horton at one point surprisingly proposed that the original manuscript and the one copy be deposited under seals in the hands of some banker, something which Moore seized on with a passion, except that his entreaties fell on deaf ears.

The burning of the Memoirs remains an act of collective vandalism and redounds badly on all, on Moore for his fecklessness in having sold the manuscript in the first place, on Hobhouse for his bogus sincerity regarding Byron's reputation and on Murray for his evident self-righteousness, describing himself as 'a tradesman determined to preserve' that reputation; on Augusta and Annabella, the silent colluders, and on the two 'executioners' Colonel Doyle and Wilmot-Horton who tore the pages from their binding and fed them to the fire. Murray called his sixteen-year-old son and heir into the room to witness the momentous piece of history. Hobhouse later claimed that he was invited to toss a few pages in but refrained from 'the pious deed' while wholeheartedly approving it. The folio sheets, bearing Byron's singular mesh-like handwriting, which Mrs Byron had paid a Mr Duncan the sum of seven shillings to tutor her son in, were swept in a fierce carnival of flame, before curdling to ash.

The ship *Florida* carrying Byron's remains arrived in England in July 1824. On board were Colonel Stanhope, Dr Bruno, Tita, Lega Zambelli, Fletcher, Benjamin the black groom and Byron's two dogs, along with Byron's trunks of books, trunks of weapons, trunks of clothes, his bed and a cache of champagne. At the London docks the undertaker broke open the tin-lined coffin and the body was transferred to a new lead coffin with the ship's flag flying above it. Hobhouse could not bear to look at his dead friend, though he did so later on when Byron lay in state in Sir Edward

Knatchbull's front parlour in Great George Street, which Hobhouse had hired in order for the streams of mourners to pay their respects. He found Byron so greatly changed as to be almost unrecognisable, while Augusta thought his expression was one of 'mocking serenity'.

Colonel Stanhope expected the state barges to come bearing dignitaries and bands to play sacred music, but he was to be sorely disappointed. Byron in death, just as in life, would suffer what John Clare called 'mildewing censure'. *The Times*, in a tempered obituary, noted that 'others were more tenderly beloved than Lord Byron', something which Hobhouse stoutly contested, saying that Byron's magical influence radiated to all who met him. *The Times* had also been precipitate in stating that Byron would be buried in Poets' Corner in Westminster Abbey, something that the Dean, Dr Ireland, who had been approached by Murray and Kinnaird, summarily scotched, and unable to repress his disgust, told them 'to carry the body away and say as little about it as possible'.

It was in the undertaker's barge with his Newfoundland dog Lyon at his feet that Byron arrived at Palace Yard Stairs, the riverbank already lined with curious spectators. Byron mania was to hit London again as it had at the height of his fame in 1812, but this time it was not in the gilded drawing rooms, it was the masses who thronged to pay their respects, believing that something of them had died with him. Tears, flowers, odes, laments and notes on black-bordered cards were strewn in that little parlour, but as Hobhouse ruefully put it, 'No one of note came.' Lit by tallow candles, Byron's coat of arms hastily painted on a wooden board, they thronged in numbers 'beyond precedent', the mêlée becoming so obstreperous that a wooden frame was erected around the bed and police sergeants called to maintain order. The number of ladies according to a newspaper was 'exceedingly great'.

The hearse, with its twelve sable plumes, drawn by six black horses, left Westminster on a warm July day, bound for the family vault at Hucknall Torkard Church, not far from Newstead Abbey in Nottinghamshire. Byron's coronet on a velvet cushion was borne by a charger which walked ahead. People flowed into the streets to bid their farewells. Hobhouse, smarting at the rejection by the Dean of Westminster, said that Byron would be buried like a nobleman, since they could not bury him like a poet, but the nobility did not share his sentiment. Of the forty-seven crest-emblazoned carriages forty-three were empty, no loyal friend from the houses of Holland, Devonshire, Melbourne or Jersey had come to mourn. Since it was not customary for women to attend funerals, Augusta was absent, but in one of life's small ironies, her husband Colonel Leigh led the cortège. Sir Ralph Noel, Annabella's father, had been invited but did not respond and the seventh Lord Byron, offended at having been omitted in Byron's will, excused himself on the grounds of ill health.

Mary Shelley, who had written in her diary that her 'dear capricious Albe' had quitted the desert world, and had gone to Great George Street to pay her respects, watched now from an upstairs window in Kentish Town, along with Jane Williams, as from all the windows people craned to see the bier of the man they knew only by hearsay. The poet John Clare, bordering on madness, seeing a beautiful young girl sigh with sorrow, thought it and the homage of the common people, the surest testament for Byron the Poet.

At St Pancras Church, where the cobblestones ran out, the empty carriages turned back. The procession took four days to reach Nottingham, mourners thronged the roadside and then at the Blackamoor's Head in Nottingham, where the remains lay in a little parlour, the crush of people was so great that a large body of constabulary had to keep order; squires, squireens and farmers come to pay their respects and according to one account, a youth bashfully recited from 'Waterloo':

> The earth is cover'd thick with other clay,
> Which her own clay shall cover, heap'd and pent,
> Rider and horse – friend, foe – in one red burial blent!

At the very same time, the memoirs of Dallas, aided by his son the Reverend Alexander, were being hurried through the printing press as an epidemic of Byron mania struck the world. The literary deification, bludgeoning and misrepresenting was now afoot. Books of gossip, smut, malice, lies and 'intrinsic nothings', as Thomas Love Peacock called them, were soon to proliferate. Peacock himself parodied Byron, giving him the name of Mr Cypress in *Nightmare Abbey*.

Fascination, envy and literary malfeasance on Byron were unceasing. Before the end of that year Southey, the Poet Laureate, in *The Quarterly Review*, accused Byron of committing 'high crime, misdemeanours against society, work in which mockery was mingled with horror, filth and impiety, profligacy with sedition and slander'. A Mr Dugdale was even more extreme, justifying his pirating of *Cain* and *Don Juan* as quite reasonable, since the works were 'so shocking and flagitious' as to be unworthy to be dignified by the word 'copyright'.

Hobhouse was wrong. They did bury him like a poet, but he resurrected as a legend. Why? we may ask. Why him above the legion of poets down the years? He was the embodiment of Everyman, human, ambitious, erratic, generous, destructive, dazzling, dark and dissonant, but yet there is the unfathomable that eludes us, and perhaps even eluded him. It is not simply that he was a poet whose poetry burst upon the world or that he was a letter-writer of consummate greatness, he reincarnates for each age as an icon with a divine spark and all-too-human flaws.

INDEX